55
SUCCESSFUL
HARVARD
LAW SCHOOL
APPLICATION
ESSAYS

55
SUCCESSFUL
HARVARD
LAW SCHOOL
APPLICATION
ESSAYS

What Worked for Them Can
Help You Get Into the Law School
of Your Choice

With Analysis by the Staff of
The Harvard Crimson

 ST. MARTIN'S GRIFFIN ❧ NEW YORK

www.stmartins.com

Library of Congress Cataloging-in-Publication Data

55 successful Harvard Law School application essays : what worked for them can help you get into the law school of your choice / with analysis by the staff of the Harvard Crimson.
      p. cm.
   ISBN-13: 978-0-312-36611-7
   ISBN-10: 0-312-36611-6
   1. Law schools—United States—Admission.   2. College applications—United States.   3. Harvard Law School—Admission.   4. Essay—Authorship.   5. Exposition (Rhetoric)   6. Academic writing.   I. Harvard crimson.   II. Title : Fifty-five successful Harvard Law School application essays.

KF285.A15 2007
340.071'17444—dc22   2007010144

First Edition: July 2007

10 9 8 7 6 5

CONTENTS

Contents

Contents

ACKNOWLEDGMENTS

Each of the fifty-five essays in this book helped its author get into Harvard Law School, one of the best law schools in the country. We at *The Harvard Crimson*, Harvard's daily newspaper, have assembled this volume in the hopes that they might also help you get into the school of your choice.

None of the essays in this book is perfect (though a few come pretty close). But each one, through its own particular strengths and flaws, holds lessons that you can apply to your own essay to take it one step closer to the best essay you can produce. The analyses by editors of the *Crimson* highlight and expand on the lessons of each essay, ensuring you get the most out of each one.

When we selected the essays that ultimately made it into this book, we kept an eye toward diversity. We have ordered the essays into six different subject areas, and even within those areas, no one essay is quite like any other. Thus, as you read the book, two things will happen. First, you'll notice that certain themes keep recurring in the essays and the analyses—giving you a better a sense of the basic elements that make for good essay writing. Second, you'll notice certain critiques that are particular to individual topics, certain strengths that help set one individual essay apart from the rest.

For making this book possible, I would like to thank, first and foremost, our editor at St. Martin's Press, David Moldawer, for the insight and motivation he provided us throughout the process. I would also like to thank Tom Mercer of St. Martin's Press, for his help in generating the idea and inspiration for the book in the first place.

This is not the first book of this kind that the *Crimson* has produced—St. Martin's Press has already published two editions of

Acknowledgments

our college essay book (*50 Successful Harvard Application Essays*), and a book featuring profiles of successful applicants to Harvard College (*How They Got Into Harvard*). So we owe gratitude to *Crimson* editors past who have paved the path in which this book walks, especially former *Crimson* presidents Matthew W. Granade (1998), Joshua H. Simon (1999), Erica K. Jalli (2004), and Lauren A. E. Schuker (2005).

Finally, I would like to thank all fifty-five law students who submitted their essays for this book. Without their creativity and skill, this book would not be possible. And, of course, the *Crimson* editors who reviewed the essays—when you took up this task, you were no experts in the field of law school essays, but you finished the product with a skill, professionalism, and attention to detail that is a testament to all of you.

—William C. Marra
President, 133rd Guard of *The Harvard Crimson*

INTRODUCTION

In 2006, nearly a hundred thousand people applied to law school in the United States. The size of the applicant pool has grown dramatically over the past decade, up nearly one third from seventy-five thousand applicants ten years ago. As competition for spots in law school classes escalates, it becomes more important than ever to find ways to set yourself apart from the pack. You must transform your application into something more than the alphabet soup of LSAT, GPA, and résumé if you want an acceptance letter from the school of your dreams. In a world where few law schools interview candidates anymore, you must find a way to convey a sense of who you are, why you want to go to law school, and why you have the makings of a great lawyer.

In other words, you have to make your mark in your personal statement.

This isn't the easiest thing to do. There is no formula for the perfect essay, no magic piece of advice to follow. The essay writing process is an intensely personal one. Your best essay will come from within you and will reflect your own goals, desires, and worldview. But this doesn't mean you cannot seek guidance in what has worked in the past.

That's where this book comes in. *55 Successful Harvard Law School Application Essays* will provide you with the tools you need to write a coherent, compelling, and unique essay that will get the attention of any law school admissions officer. The essays we've compiled here, all of which helped earn their authors a seat at Harvard Law School, will familiarize you with the subjects and writing styles that admissions officers at one of the country's most competitive law schools look for. We have paired each essay with a review written by an editor of *The*

Introduction

Harvard Crimson, Harvard's daily newspaper, assessing the piece's strengths and weaknesses.

We recognize that these essays were just one part of applications that likely included stunning test scores, GPAs, and résumés, and it is difficult to determine how much weight an essay carried in its writer's acceptance. As such, some of our reviewers have taken a very critical eye to these "successful" essays to talk about how the writers could have further improved their personal statements. We hope these tougher appraisals will guide you in your own writing process and remind you of some of the pitfalls of the personal essay. Not even the perfect essay can ensure a placement in Harvard's next law school class, but it certainly helps present a more compelling argument of why you deserve to get in.

When you read the essays and their analyses, two things should become apparent. First, your writing style and ability to effectively communicate a convincing argument are critical. Remember that, above all else, admissions officers are looking for clear thinkers who can convincingly advance a claim. The way you write your essay and craft your argument is key. The admissions officers are the first jury you'll face in your law career, so make your opening statement a powerful one.

Second, your essay topic is vitally important. You get to make only one statement, so choose the set of experiences or beliefs that best represents who you are and what you value. We have grouped the essays in this book into six broad categories. These groupings are a useful starting point as you begin to develop your essay. Think about which category your experiences best fit, and keep the overarching theme in the back of your head throughout your essay writing. Here are the categories:

- **Constructing Your Identity:** Personal statements are obviously intended to be personal. Discussing your cultural identity and heritage is often the most effective way to tell an admissions officer who you are and to get beyond the test scores and course grades on your transcript.

- **Words and Language:** The study of law is all about understanding and interpreting language and the written word. The authors of the essays in this category love language and explore its cultural, political, and legal impact. If you have ever studied a foreign language or have even simply been moved by an especially eloquent bumper sticker, this might be the category for you.

- **"I Want to Be a Lawyer Because . . .":** There's a reason you're going to law school, right? Essays in this category give the admissions officer a clear sense of why the applicant is applying to law school and, more importantly, what type of law he or she wants to practice, whether it be international law or local tax law.

- **Travels:** One of the lessons of this book is that sometimes we learn best by studying others. The authors of the essays in this category write about the life and legal lessons they learned while studying or working abroad. This genre, which often features compelling and colorful anecdotes, makes for some of the most captivating reads.

- **Climbing the Mountain:** Nothing demonstrates your character better than overcoming adversity. Scaling mountains, both figurative and literal, and surviving a test of character to fight another day are popular essay topics at all levels. Law school is no exception. Study the way these essays are written to figure how to best tell the story of the time you slew Goliath.

- **An Intellectual Desire:** The authors in this category have not forgotten that law school is, well, three years of school. You will be learning a lot and will likely be in the most rigorous academic environment you have ever experienced. These writers discuss the academic draw of law school and the source of their intellectual thirst for legal knowledge.

Introduction

Whether you read this book from start to finish, or jump around looking for the essay that will give you the eureka moment you are seeking, I hope you enjoy the journey. I wish you the very best of luck writing your essay and getting into the law school that's right for you.

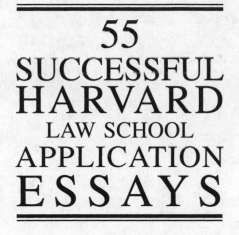

55
SUCCESSFUL
HARVARD
LAW SCHOOL
APPLICATION
ESSAYS

CONSTRUCTING YOUR IDENTITY

KENNETH BASIN

They had been subjected to indignity after indignity. They had paid over six months' salary per person for the "privilege" of relinquishing their Soviet citizenship (though conveniently enough, they had lost their jobs upon applying for their visas and being labeled *refusniks*). They had stood quietly as armed soldiers barraged them with accusations of treason, anti-Semitic slurs, and threats of imprisonment. But standing in that train station in the Ukrainian border town of Chop, waiting for the train that would take them out of the Soviet Union and on the first leg of their journey to the United States, my parents had finally had enough: they would not let a book of *Grimm's Fairy Tales* go. The Russian customs official who made the final inspection of their bags had removed only the book, leaving my parents grateful that they had gotten off rather easily. But as they started toward the train platform, my sister (then five years old) lingered behind, growing increasingly hysterical at the loss of her favorite book. My father pled with the official, not as a *refusnik* to a soldier or a Jew to an ethnic Russian, but as one father to another, for the return of his daughter's beloved book.

It was November 22, 1981, and my parents and sister boarded their train westward with two suitcases of clothing, $210 in cash, and a book of *Grimm's Fairy Tales*. Though I was not yet born, it is a story I have to come to know and feel as deeply as any of my own.

In my experience, it is in the home that one's eyes are first opened to the outside world, and my parents saw to it from early on that my eyes were wide open. With a family that had immigrated as political refugees to the United States, arriving in January 1982, international affairs took on a whole new life within my home. The end of the Cold War and the collapse of the Soviet Union were more than headlines my father read in the newspaper; they were personal experiences shared by every member of my family.

When I began my studies at the University of Southern California, then, I never doubted that my cosmopolitan interests would find a way to express themselves. I set out on a study-abroad program to London in January 2004 in search of the one lesson I felt that USC, or any American university, could never truly offer me: perspective.

And so it was that on my summer break in Europe after attending King's College London, I found myself retracing my parents' experiences through the continent on their way to the United States. In Eastern Europe, the legacy of Soviet Cold War domination allowed me to communicate using my proficiency in conversational Russian. In Bratislava, I arrived by train at the same station that received my parents' train from Chop. In Vienna, I passed by the palace where for six days my parents were held under armed guard to protect them from terrorists who had been targeting Jews and other refugees from the east in the winter of 1981. In Rome, I strolled through the neighborhood where my parents spent three weeks, waiting for their visas to enter the United States to clear.

Given my experience with my family, my interest in international law comes as little surprise. When I consider the challenges my parents faced in the repressive climate of the U.S.S.R. during the Cold War, as well as those they confronted in trying to escape it, the vitality of the field takes on a whole new salience for me: the modern world is a deeply interconnected one, and with that interconnection comes an underlying sense of uncertainty. If man is to survive that uncertainty, he must find in it a guiding order. In my mind, international law is the means by which humanity can find that essential order and, with it, the stability and progress necessary to thrive.

Constructing Your Identity

In the end, I have come to feel very strongly that the whole world is my home and, more than that, my responsibility. From the twinkling lights of Paris to the dusty corridors of one-time communist Budapest, from the bustle and excitement of the Turkish bazaar to the natural peace and beauty of Australia's Great Barrier Reef, I have long believed that the world is my classroom. I have very much enjoyed attending class.

Review by Emma Lind

This essay's effectiveness rests in its deeply personal nature. Because Kenneth's interest in international law can be understood only in terms of his family history, it could not have been written by anyone else. The fact that he is able to communicate the profundity of his family's escape from political oppression with clarity and concision, and then spin that into his personal draw to the field of law, is what makes this essay dexterous and strong.

The first sentence of the essay is punchy, essential to grabbing a law school admissions officer's attention and ensuring that [he or she] remember[s] the essay when comparing [Kenneth's] application to others. The introductory paragraph delivers what the first sentence promises: a gripping story that is universally fascinating but holds enough personal elements to give it a raw authenticity. This is the strongest paragraph in the essay, as it communicates the author's ability to synthesize information he heard from his parents and establish both a historical context for it and a deep personal connection to it.

The second and third paragraphs clearly transition the essay from a story of [Kenneth's] family to a story of himself. His mention of study in London gives purpose to his decision to go abroad, which would appear on his transcript without any context or explanation. Notice also how he mentions that he speaks Russian, and communicates his interest and dedication to history, without being ostentatious about it. He mentions law only at the end of the essay, but the connection is strong enough that his conviction comes off as confident and to the point. Kenneth, however, could have done more with his last sentence, which is trite and doesn't draw on a theme present throughout the essay. He should have mentioned his family history again to bring the essay full circle.

NICOLE DOOLEY

It usually takes people several attempts to figure me out. With the toffee-colored skin and curly hair that I inherited from my black father and Puerto Rican mother, my racial heritage has never been easy to guess. I've been assumed to be white, black, Hispanic, South Asian, and Middle Eastern, to name a few. With my background so hard to place, I could fit quite nicely into the predominantly white suburbs where I grew up. I didn't look or feel all that different from the Dohertys or the Barravecchios living there. The racial homogeneity of my upbringing had an unfortunate side effect: I never had an opportunity to connect with black or Hispanic culture outside of my family. Growing up, I didn't really notice. Acute racial awareness did not hit me until college.

At that point, Rice University was the most diverse place I had ever lived. At first, I spent my free time with my South Asian and white roommates, as I was not ready to explore the black and Hispanic groups on campus. Soon enough, though, I ventured out, hoping they would add a sense of belonging to my life that I thought was lacking. I joined the Black Student Association, eager to find my niche. Instead, at every meeting or event I attended, I stayed on the outskirts, feeling separated, as if I were observing through a glass wall. I couldn't commiserate about being racially profiled, and I could get my hair wet whenever I wanted. My feelings of disappointment were so cutting that I didn't attempt a single foray into the Hispanic group on campus. As someone who didn't speak Spanish fluently, I feared that I would feel similarly disconnected.

By the time I graduated from Rice, I had decided to take steps to grow into my ethnicity. To begin this journey, I spent three weeks in Puerto Rico. My intent was to speak only Spanish for the duration of the trip and lose myself in the culture. Unfortunately for me, everyone on the island spoke English and could tell my Spanish was not up to par as soon as the first anglicized *hola* came out of my mouth. As for culture, I felt oddly unexposed. My relatives took me to all the tourist spots and malls, where the customs mirrored those of the white neighborhoods where I had been raised. Ultimately, my trip brought me no closer to identifying with my Hispanic heritage, and I returned to the States disappointed.

The next part of my journey involved my postgraduation plans: teaching in inner-city Atlanta. I did not pick this path so that I could explore my "blackness," but it was a fortunate side effect. I saw the experience as an opportunity to connect with and learn about African American culture—my culture. From the start, my seventh graders branded me as an outsider by not referring to me as light-skinned, their sign of acceptance. Instead, I was white. I quickly learned that to them, being black was less of a genetic fact and more of an attitude, which I initially lacked. The rejection I felt fully eclipsed the disconnection I felt in college. However, necessity is the mother of invention, and I needed my students to accept me in order to achieve my goals of racial acceptance and effective teaching. As each day passed, I related to them a little more by spending time with them at school and at their homes, both during the week and on the weekends. By the end of the year, my students serenaded me with songs about their light-skinned teacher. My personal quest for ethnicity was over; my students had taught me how to belong.

Part of my duty as their teacher was to return the favor by teaching them how to belong in the world outside their inner-city neighborhood.

Unfortunately, I was unable to give my students a complete picture of their greater surroundings within the confines of the classroom. I realized that in order to help my students, I needed to go beyond the classroom into the realm of law. Many of the obstacles preventing them from attaining a complete education stemmed from issues within the legal system, such as the emphasis placed on standardized testing. An understanding of law and policy making will give me a greater basis to provide minority students with resources to reach beyond their borders to their fullest potential. I not only want to understand the existing law, but I also aim to make laws more equitable and fair for my former students. Law school will better equip me to give them the opportunity to expand their horizons, as I had done.

Review by April Yee

Several hundred words is precious real estate, especially when the stakes are entrance to Harvard Law. Dooley writes a compelling essay that shows the reader she aims to serve an underprivileged population, and a reader would have benefited from more details about her experience teaching in inner-city Atlanta.

Dooley shines in the second half of her essay. When she tells the reader that she visited students at their homes, she shows that she cares about her students and about being a good teacher. "By the end of the year, my students serenaded me with songs about their light-skinned teacher," she writes, giving proof that her students appreciated her efforts.

In her final paragraph, she explains how learning law will help her to serve her students. Now the reader knows why Dooley's quest for a racial identity and her love for her students matters.

Still, the essay could be improved if she used her limited essay space to detail her experiences. She could have recounted her first day on the job, described the inside of a student's inner-city home, or recalled the words to the songs her students sang to her. Dooley leaves the reader wanting to know more and feeling as if they're missing some vital information—something that may make for a good murder mystery, but not a good law-school application essay.

HANI N. ELIAS

Growing up, I was frequently reminded by my parents—sometimes casually over dinner, sometimes with more religious undertones after Sunday Mass—that an abbot of a monastery had once predicted my monastic future. As an infant I was baptized into the Coptic Orthodox Church in a monastery founded in the fourth century by Saint Antony. The twenty-year-old Antony, meditating on the meaning of this temporary life after the passing of his wealthy parents, heeded the commandment of Christ to a rich man in the Gospel of Matthew and escaped into the Sahara: "If thou wishest to be perfect, go and sell everything which thou hast, give to the poor, and take thy cross, and come after Me, and there shall be unto thee treasure in heaven." As a young Christian, I admired Saint Antony for his self-sacrifice, but that was the extent of thought I gave to monasticism. Occupied with school and extracurricular commitments, comforted by my parents and friends, I saw meditation as an ambition for those with loftier sensibilities.

Spring semester of my junior year at Harvard, however, tested me in unique and unfamiliar ways. I often found myself unable to focus in class, crying alone in my room, and unable to laugh at even the funniest moments from *Seinfeld*. A flood of thoughts distracted me, but a recurring one would eventually lead me back to the monastery, this time in the guise of a scholar. I kept asking myself: despite my seeming academic success and comfortable life, why do I feel so unhappy, so out of place in the midst of common surroundings? I visited a number of physicians but the traditional medical lexicon could not describe my ailments and preoccupations; I called my parents daily but, unable to fully understand my problems, we could only pray together. I felt helpless at times and endlessly frustrated. This struggle pushed me to study monasticism for my senior honors thesis. My research focused on notions of world abnegation. I wanted to explore the plausibility of living independent of material possessions and from a technological and economic order that is leaving more and more people discontented, reliant on antidepressants, and in a chronic state of stress.

On August 1, 2004, I made my way to California's Mojave Desert where, between Los Angeles and Las Vegas, seven monks live in cenobitic life in a small Coptic monastery. Despite an intense heat, I immediately felt an inner sense of calm and peace. Surrounded by mountains and disturbed by neither penetrating buildings nor offensive billboards, here I had the opportunity to discover myself; here my soul could refresh itself. The desert, as I once heard before, truly appeared to me as a plane between earth and heaven. Aside from my fascination with this dry wilderness, I was astonished to discover that an ethic of brotherliness breathed life into this desolate landscape. In the monastery, it would be inappropriate for anyone to go to bed upset with another member of the community; after our evening prayer, it became routine to reconcile any personal differences by kissing each other's hands and asking for forgiveness. And yet behind this outward layer of monastic culture, I soon discovered a more disquieting ethos. A week into my spiritual retreat and academic journey, I read a disturbing message from an early church father on the wall of a monk's cell: he exhorts us not to fear the dead but to "run away from the living." To a monk, this short message accurately conveys a central precept of monasticism, but to me it somehow equally contradicted my innermost vision of my own sense of place amidst the community and larger world.

The monks' disengagement from the troubles of the outside world was especially upsetting to me because of a trip I had taken to Egypt three years before. In one town, I experienced a poverty to which neither books nor even photographs could fully do justice. Ezbet el Nakhl, an area inhabited by the city's garbage collectors, was, to an adolescent who was by no means wealthy, hell on earth. I interacted with youth my own age whose sole arenas of play were heads of garbage; I smelled an unbelievable odor; and most disturbing, I encountered parents and children who no longer believed that things would ever improve. I keep thinking that these living beings, effectively ignored not only by their corrupt government but also by monks, deserve my attention. The ethic of brotherliness and the principle of compassion—notions common within the monastery—cannot help those struggling to eat or escape disease so long as they remain limited to interactions between solitaries and recluses.

Recognizing the importance of the mores of monastic communities, namely, selfless love and brotherliness, it has been my passion to create a network of globally conscious students—future leaders who are committed to serving and helping those less privileged. In 2002, I founded CollegeCorps, a national nonprofit organization whose mission is to remove obstacles that currently prevent undergraduate students from becoming involved in health, education, and environmental work in resource-poor countries. While providing financial assistance and practical training to students alone may not alleviate poverty and disease, my stay in the monastery helped me realize that I cannot turn my back on those who are repeatedly marginalized. Perhaps paradoxically, I have also come to value asceticism. Like Antony, at twenty, I aspire to internalize the principle of self-sacrifice, to avoid the paralysis of a lukewarm passion. Rather than escaping into remoteness, I will apply this rich ethic as I help those who face poverty and those who suffer from disease.

Review by Emma Lind

The strength of this essay is that the applicant manages to discuss a very impressive part of his résumé (starting CollegeCorps) without just regurgitating a list of his accomplishments. From the essay, it is clear that founding CollegeCorps was a turning point in the author's life, and he discusses it by giving background about his personal life and struggles, and then relating that to why he wants to help people. His essay does not specifically say why he wants to attend law school, but it doesn't have to—the tone and content of his essay indicate his reasons for him.

His first sentence grabs the reader's attention by revealing his supposed religious vocation, unusual in the largely secular world of law school applications. This up-front and unashamed individuality is key when admissions officers are reading thousands of applications from similarly qualified applicants. The first paragraph is strong because it steers away from the tempting but detrimental "I want to go law school because . . ." trap.

The applicant delves into the deeply revealing and personal in the second paragraph, setting a tone of complete honesty and personal awareness. The last sentence demonstrates his ability to tie in his academic prowess to his personal interest in religion and emotional struggles, which speaks well of his intellectual abilities.

The rest of the essay reveals that the applicant is a gifted writer and communicator while transitioning flawlessly from his personal saga with religion and academics to his growing awareness of his place in the larger world community. The end of the second-to-last paragraph and the beginning of the last paragraph form the core of his essay: a personal account of how a previous conviction proved to be unfulfilling, and explaining his subsequent turn to an interest in law. The end of the last paragraph, though, is a bit too much: comparing oneself to a saint is almost always something to avoid.

SARAH HYMAN

Famous for little except their smoked salmon, ponies, and the Fair Isle sweater pattern, the Shetland Islands are not the sort of place one often hears about. Perched in the North Sea halfway between Scotland and Norway, the Shetlands belong to Scotland thanks to a dowry from Christian I of Norway in 1468. Since the time of the Vikings, a Norse language had been spoken in Shetland; the handover to Scotland, however, spelled doom for this fringe Scandinavian tongue known as Norn. As Scots English became the language of government and church, there was little need for the increasingly dated and old-fashioned Norn. I never would have heard of Norn if it were not for a single line of a linguistics article I read during the spring of my junior year, in my private tutorial with Professor Jay Jasanoff. The article mentioned in passing that the current dialect of the Shetland Islands was in fact Scots English mixed with a heavy infusion of Norn, whose last speakers died in the eighteenth century. Intrigued by this exotic combination of English and Norse, I wondered about the current status of the Shetland dialect and how much of it consisted of remnants from the Norn era. Always up for an academic scavenger hunt, I began, with the approval and guidance of Professor Jasanoff, to scour Harvard's libraries for all they held on the Shetlands and their strange amalgamation of Norse and Scots.

Especially intriguing to me and unusual for a spoken vernacular, the Shetland dialect, as I discovered, had been used without self-consciousness by generations of Shetlanders in both casual and formal social settings. The twentieth century, however, heralded the discovery of oil in the North Sea; consequently, both money and nonnative workers flowed into the Shetlands, the latter of which pushed the Shetland dialect along a path toward extinction.

Having decided to focus my thesis on the steps Shetlanders were taking to prevent the death of their dialect, I traveled to Shetland in May 2003 thanks to a grant from the Harvard College Research

Program. While there, I found that Islanders no longer needed to speak their dialect since the predominance of "southmouthers" from mainland Britain meant that Shetland residents frequently spoke Standard British and Scots English. It also became clear to me that those who were trying to promote the Shetland dialect did so because of its emotional importance: no longer necessary for communication, the Shetland dialect with its Norn remnants was actually a living embodiment of [the Islanders'] Scandinavian heritage.

This notion that people can, through efforts to organize language promotion programs, prevent or slow down a dialect's march toward the grave . . . fascinated me. For centuries languages had died with little fanfare as there was always a new dialect or language in use to take its place. As Professor Michael Barnes of the University College London wrote, "The concept of language as a badge of personal identity seems only to have become widespread in the nineteenth century, and . . . tended chiefly to excite those with the leisure to ponder such matters."[1] Thus, the fact that some Shetlanders were proposing laws to require Shetland dialect instruction in schools stands as evidence of a new awareness of language as an important element in identity: though Shetlanders had no trouble communicating in Standard English, there existed a sentimental motive to keep the Shetland dialect alive. By relying on the legal system to effect linguistic change, Shetlanders reveal a belief that nearly all facets of human behavior can be shaped through legal means—even requiring that a dying dialect be spoken in schools.

After assessing Shetland's actual language promotion efforts through fieldwork, interviews, and library research, I concluded that the Shetland dialect, although emotionally valuable, was destined to die. Parents, who wanted their children to learn Standard English so they could attend university in mainland Britain, thought that teaching the dialect in schools was preposterous. Furthermore, although many Shetlanders

---

[1]Michael P. Barnes, *The Norn Language of Orkney and Shetland* (Lerwick: Shetland Times, 1998), 25.

were sad to see the dialect abandoned, most did not take any initiative to organize a dialect promotion program. Although Shetlanders indeed thought of their dialect as a badge of personal identity, it did not appear to be one worth protecting.

Upon my return from the Shetlands, Professor Jasanoff suggested that I compare the situation in the Shetlands to other European minority-language promotions. Thinking that rescuing a language through legal means was somewhat unnatural, I did not expect to find many successful linguistic promotion efforts. Surprisingly, citizens of both Luxembourg and the Faroe Islands successfully organized movements to promote their native languages. The Shetland dialect movement, I then realized, will likely fail because of the particular indifference among Shetlanders, not because it is inherently untenable to promote a language/dialect through legal channels.

What had started as a project investigating the fragile state of the Shetland dialect ended with my examination of how modern legal systems and motivated civic groups can alter language use. After having a small taste of how the law shapes its citizens, I plan to pursue a much more detailed examination of the written words that were crafted to dictate our behavior. After all, the law is the ultimate arena for linguistic study: nowhere else do words have as much power, and in no other context can an ambiguous sentence have more impact. I am looking forward to spending the next three years and beyond immersed in a world of these influential words.

Review by Bari M. Schwartz

From the opening sentence, Sarah's application essay is striking with its unique anecdotes, successful demonstration of her passions and work ethic, and overall quality of writing. Rather than stating all of this as fact, Sarah allows them to appear organically through the essay's construction. The writing is anything but boring, as Sarah takes the reader along on her academic and personal quest.

The essay's structure, in which she first presents her interest in language and concludes by illustrating how law and language intersect, is a formula overused in law-school admissions essays. Regardless, the essay's assets outweigh its formulaic structure, and her essay still stands out among the numerous other essays that attempt to do the same thing.

Sarah's inclusion of a quote with a footnote may not have been the wisest choice—the essay temporarily breaks from its memoir style and risks becoming too academic and impersonal. Also, it just takes too long to read through the essay—Sarah could have been a little more judicious in deciding just how many anecdotes and facts to include. The reader has to plod through a lot of material to discover why she wants to attend law school, and specifically Harvard.

Sarah's writing attests to her talent and her love for language, but her interest in law school is not obvious. The essay could just as well be an application for graduate study in linguistics. Further discussion of Sarah's interest in studying law itself would better serve the purpose of the personal statement.

BRENDEN MILLSTEIN

Let me tell you about my friend Jake, the trumpet player. He hung out with the wrong kids. He was caught drinking on campus and was suspended. Then he was caught smoking pot on campus and was suspended. He was arrested for robbery and thrown in juvenile hall my sophomore year. All the parents in the Jazz Ensemble signed a letter of support and faith in Jake and sent the letter to the judge. Jake was let out of juvenile hall, under the mandate that he was to stay in Ensemble. Within a week, he got into a fight. Some of his teeth were knocked out.

Constructing Your Identity

It was the best thing that ever happened to him. He couldn't play trumpet for weeks and realized that something in his life had to change. He started hanging out with new friends and rearranged his life. He was back in the Ensemble in a few weeks. The next year I saw him prevent fights, and break up fights after they had begun. Now he goes to Cal State San Jose, where he has had no disciplinary problems.

Let me tell you about my friend Ted. He has no parents and is being raised by his single grandmother. He won the Yamaha National Drum Competition against college students when he was nine years old. One day he did not come to Ensemble. The day before, the gang he hung out with was the target of a drive-by shooting. He hid beneath a car. He was too afraid to come to school the next day. He stopped hanging out with the gang. When he was a sophomore in high school, he was awarded a full scholarship to Berklee College of Music. Now he attends Berklee when he is not on tour.

Let me tell you about my friend Joe, the drummer. He lived in Concord and every day commuted fifty minutes each way to Berkeley High, so he could play drums in the Jazz Ensemble. His drum set was stolen. His family started saving money to buy another drum set. Then his house burned down. Now he lives in Oakland, another long commute, and does not own a drum set. His junior year, he won a full scholarship to Berklee College of Music. He is the drummer on the CD I produced; he played on a borrowed set of drums.

Let me tell you about my friend Tony. He was arrested for defacing public property his sophomore year. He was held in juvenile hall for two days. Several weeks later, he escaped the police by jumping a fence topped with barbed wire. He cut his hands and could not play trumpet for three weeks. This was a turning point for him. Now he avoids all hard drugs and paints in a sketchbook. He does not fail classes anymore. He practices several hours a day and has a direction to his life.

What has Ensemble meant to me? Every day in Ensemble, I work with Ted, Joe, Jake, and Tony. And I work with everyone else in the band. After four years in the band, I have become friends with all of them. Through them I have seen many different sides of life. What has this experience meant to me? It has changed the way I look at life. I no longer take anything for granted. Every day in Ensemble I am reminded that I am lucky, not because my parents are together, but because I have parents at all. Every day I am reminded that I am lucky because I have never had to worry about getting shot while hanging out with my friends. Every day I am reminded that I am lucky because I don't have to worry about having enough to eat. I love life. I love life no matter what, because I see every day how much worse it could be. But I also see joy in the musicians' lives. All of us love music. And when we play, everyone's troubles are forgotten. Or if not forgotten, expressed, and so released through the music. When the Ensemble plays, our various backgrounds combine to form an incredible mosaic of music. And I love it. And everyone else in the band loves it. And most people listening love it too, for whether or not they understand the music, they can feel the energy. And for a few moments, everyone is truly, genuinely happy. What has playing in the Ensemble meant to me? It has shown me a release from sorrow, from anger, from fear. It has shown me a bonding of people and of cultures. It has shown me that it is an insult to others to take anything for granted. It has shown me how to express myself in a way that can be understood by musicians anywhere. It has shown me how to work with people and, more important, how to become friends with them. It has given me a window into other cultures, other backgrounds, and other lives, and it has given me a window into myself.

Ensemble has also given me a way to help. I organize and lead a quartet: drums, bass, piano, and me, sax. We get gigs around the Bay Area, $300 to $500 per gig. All our earnings go to the Ensemble scholarship fund. The fund is for instruments, lessons, and tour costs. The Ensemble has an "all-or-nothing" policy for tours—everyone goes or nobody goes. Many of the musicians cannot afford to pay any tour costs, and most cannot afford to pay all of the costs. My combo raises thousands of dollars for the fund. It feels good to play with members of the Ensemble, and it feels good when my combo gets paid and a new trombone appears in class the next week.

Review by William C. Marra

Brenden has written a wonderful essay here, thanks to a fantastic writing style that allows him to make the most of a very compelling story. Repetition is at the core of this essay, especially the formulation "Let me tell you about my friend." This writing device gives the reader a sense that his friends' difficulties are everywhere in Brenden's life—everyone has them, and they are all part of the same system. Meanwhile, the short sentences Brenden uses when describing their hardships lend a sense of inevitability to their troubles. There is no attempt to rationalize what has happened—it just is. Notice also that Brenden structures his essay into three separate parts. Normally you do not want to segment your essay into too many parts, but with this particular essay it works well, as each part serves a distinct function in the essay.

This essay is unique because its focus is not on the author. Brenden does not talk about himself, but others, and he comes in only insofar as he is friends with these people. In a stack of essays filled with students talking about their accomplishments and strengths, Brenden's will stand out as written by a humble man who understands that he has much to learn from others, even those nearer to the bottom of the social ladder. If you plan to write about some obstacle you have overcome or difficult circumstance you have had to deal with, consider approaching the essay by focusing on the other people who shared those circumstances, and then bringing yourself in at the end.

DANIEL PIERCE

Aeropuerto. My love of language began with this single word. After my first day of high-school Spanish, I lay on my bed with my book propped on my chest and carefully repeated it over and over. My tongue stumbled maddeningly over the word's flapped "r" sounds and strings of unruly vowels, but I was determined to pronounce it correctly. For most other students at my small high school in rural eastern Tennessee, the foreign-language requirement was a hurdle standing between them and their diplomas. While the places beyond our region interested few people I knew, other cultures fascinated me from a very young age. One of my favorite childhood pastimes was spinning my globe and imagining what life was like in the unpronounceable cities my finger landed on, and my first Spanish class represented an opportunity to discover more about the people in those exotic faraway places. On that afternoon seven years ago, I spent over an hour on my bed repeating the word *aeropuerto* until I was satisfied that I had it right. Since that day, I have had an insatiable passion for language.

Determination to master a single word soon developed into a general resolve to acquire as many words in other languages as possible. I am one of the peculiar people who consider mastering the Cyrillic alphabet or researching Romance-language pronoun evolution a good time. Languages amaze me in their staggering complexity yet striking simplicity—while they are dauntingly complex systems of rules and exceptions to me, any small child can master them without training. Studying other tongues has given me a fuller understanding of the way languages, including my own, function. I now have increased awareness and control over the manner in which I express myself in English (though perhaps, according to my friends, on occasion I tend to overanalyze what others say).

As any student of foreign languages can attest, the pursuit of fluency is a never-ending challenge. My many blunders (calling myself a "pig" instead of a "left-hander") and embarrassing moments (enduring correction from a five-year-old) have caused me to consider giving up many times. However, the personal relationships I have developed with people from other countries as a result of our shared language have made the effort worthwhile. I will never forget the delight of my Bangladeshi roommate's mother when I greeted her in Bengali or the astonishment of a Moroccan man when I conversed with him in both French and Arabic. Participating in a massive antiterrorism demonstration in the rain-soaked streets of Madrid two days after the train bombings there made me very thankful I had studied Spanish. My exposure to people from the places I used to dream about has given me a broader perspective on the world. Teaching English to local Hispanics allowed me to see the other side of our country's immigration debate through the eyes of the poor Mexican migrant workers who became my friends. By studying Arabic and rooming with a Muslim, I have developed a respect for the Islamic faith and more acceptance for differing religious views than my background as a Southern Baptist pastor's son afforded me.

My interest in other languages eventually evolved into a desire to explore deeper questions concerning the way language works and the role it plays in human life. Through my self-designed major in linguistics, I have viewed language as a way of examining both humanity and the world through disciplines as disparate as philosophy, anthropology, and computer science. Language is the vehicle for transmission of our culture, the medium of expression for our thoughts and ideas, and the basis for human society. The intellectual rigor and logical nature of language's scientific study interest me, but in the end I find examining language from the outside unfulfilling. Linguistics seeks to explore the connection between language, society, and the individual, but its status as a detached observer prevents it from affecting those relationships.

Experience speaking other languages has taught me to value the shared, profoundly human, action of communicating with others to understand their views and formulate my own. At the same time, my study of linguistics has allowed me to appreciate language as an object of extreme complexity that demands thorough analysis. Because of my interest in these two very different aspects of language, I now feel compelled to seek a career in the field of law. At its core, the study of the law is the study of language and the way it can be used to establish and modify the framework for human interaction. Through language, the law seeks a consensus of views in order to codify the rules that govern all of us. While both linguistics and the law engage in the common activity of examining language's complexities, the law does so with the express purpose of using language as a tool to change society. By studying the law, I look forward to continuing to challenge my beliefs through interaction with others and to studying more profoundly the phenomenon that has fascinated me from the day I learned *aeropuerto*.

Review by Bari M. Schwartz

Daniel Pierce does not do himself much of a favor with this essay on his love of language. The entire essay unoriginally describes his love of language, and his reasoning does not set him apart from anyone else who loves studying foreign languages. And the motif does tend to get overused for applications to both law school and other undergraduate and graduate institutions.

The reason Daniel is unconvincing is that he doesn't provide the reader with new insight about learning a language. It is clear to anyone who has studied a foreign language that language intersects with culture; that languages are complex; that an adult student will still know less than a five-year-old for whom the language is his native tongue; and that learning languages helps foster international relationships.

Toward the middle, Daniel makes reference to his Bangladeshi roommate's mother. Had he started instead with an anecdote about this situation, one unique to him as opposed to the discovery of a "single word" (a cliché opening line in itself), perhaps he would have better grabbed the reader's attention. Instead, this one-line story seems gratuitous. Furthermore, *aeropuerto*—the word that ostensibly ties the entire essay together—does not take on any special meaning. If, for example, his essay segued into an anecdote about a layover in a Mexican airport and his run-in with the law's intersection with international relations, this would have made a much more intriguing and convincing essay.

Daniel's focus on explaining language unfortunately gives the reader only limited insight into his personality, previous experiences, or why he is so personally compelled to study law.

ALLISON RONE

White. It is just one word, five letters, a mere syllable, yet it categorizes the ethnicity of over two-thirds of the American population. I check its box on standardized tests, job applications, and demographic questionnaires quite regularly, but every time I pause, conscious of a vague resentment that the label stirs in the recesses of my mind.

You see, though "white" may describe the color of my skin, it tells nothing of my background, my culture, or the rich heritage my family brought to America less than a century ago. It is a legacy that I have fought hard to revive and preserve, part of my identity that I feel is cheapened by our society's blanket Caucasian moniker. I am not merely white—I am Norwegian, a distinction to which I ascribe considerable importance.

My heritage did not always play such a pivotal role in my life. When my ancestors emigrated from Norway in the early twentieth century, they strove to assimilate into their new homeland, to be "white" instead of foreign. They encouraged their children to speak English, wear American clothing, eat American foods, and otherwise forget the country they left behind. In a single generation, they succeeded. Neither my mother nor my father grew up understanding the

Norwegian language, and until a few years ago, they knew little of Norwegian culture and traditions.

As a child with a diverse array of friends, many of whom lived in homes where their ethnicities were actively celebrated, I became increasingly aware of my comparative lack of heritage. I watched my peers preserve their ancestral cultures with a touch of jealousy, longing to know and appreciate my own background. I was not satisfied with being just "white." I wanted to find something unique about myself and my family's past, something that could differentiate me from my classmates. Unfortunately, my parents and grandparents were no help; having grown up with no awareness of their heritage, the questions I asked them about our family's history were met with shrugs or vague memories at best.

Taking matters into my own hands, as a young teenager I decided to attend Skogfjorden, a Norwegian-language camp in Bemidji, Minnesota, that promised to immerse me in all things Norwegian for four wonderful weeks. I spent every summer during high school there, studying the language, literature, and culture of my ancestral land while earning three high-school credits for my academic work. In an unexpected yet welcome concurrence, I came home from those summers to a progressively more Norwegian home. My newfound knowledge of and enthusiasm for Norway and its traditions spread among my immediate family members upon my return each year, and together we integrated them into our daily lives. Scandinavian desserts at Christmas, Norwegian blessings before dinner, traditional costumes, fireworks on May 17 (Norway's independence day); bit by bit, our home began to reestablish itself as a Norwegian American household.

Upon leaving for college, I continued to actively seek information about my heritage. I enrolled in as many courses as possible related to Scandinavia, studying topics that ranged from the Old Norse sagas to modern Scandinavian international relations. My interest deepened commensurate with my knowledge as I delved deeper into the colorful history from which Norway had emerged—folklore, mythology, kings and queens, heroes and explorers, ancient texts, rune stones, and legends. At the same time, I had the good fortune to make the acquaintance of a few Norwegian exchange students who supplemented my formal schoolwork with their firsthand accounts of modern Norway and its youth culture.

Yet for all my studies I still knew very little of my personal Norwegian history, a shortcoming that I felt compelled to remedy. So, during the summer between my first and second years at Harvard, I finally traveled to Norway itself. The three weeks I spent there could not have been a more perfect complement to my years of academic and extramural study. I hiked on mountains I had read of in the sagas, saw the ruins of Viking ships, ate hearty Norwegian food, toured the parliament building in Oslo, and practiced the language constantly. Most importantly, I paid a long-overdue visit to my Norwegian relatives, those whom my forefathers had left behind. Their joy at my arrival and eagerness to share their way of life, the way of life that I had sought so fervently to understand and imitate over the years, overwhelmed me. Only after many happy tears and many long conversations into the night—for, after all, we had decades of catching up to do—did I leave with promises not to lose touch again, promises that have since been kept and that I am certain will never be broken.

In the years since that visit, I have persisted in seeking opportunities to learn about and participate in my heritage. From the experience of my parents and grandparents, I appreciate how quickly inattention can stifle a family legacy, and I am determined not to repeat their mistake. I still have much to discover about Norway and my past, but I think I can safely say that I will never be simply "white" again. Though the color of my skin remains the same, my sense of self has changed forever.

Review by Annie M. Lowrey

Imagine the glee the admissions officer slogging through dozens of droll and polite papers must feel when she comes upon this. With cavalier counterintuition and assertiveness, the essay seizes upon the superheated topic of race in America and makes a pointed claim. And over the course of the essay, the writer convincingly shows why her Norwegian American heritage supersedes the "white" label that society applies to her.

The stakes are high. Had the writer stumbled in convincing us of the importance of her heritage, she risks seeming, well, bigoted, self-aggrandizing, contrary, and reactionary. Due to these heightened stakes, the essay works best in its bold first paragraphs. The single word of the opening sentence grips the reader's attention, and the ensuing argument tumbles conventional wisdom on its head. It's exciting stuff. And the writer does well to move beyond her original claim and nuance her argument; she persuades the reader that identifying her Norwegian heritage meant not only breaking from the Caucasian fold but also [developing] a deeper self-actualization.

Because the beginning of the essay demonstrated such fire with its hard aphorisms, the middle and end seem a bit wet in comparison; the essay dwindles to a final trite comment. The writer cedes to the common pitfall of telling instead of showing, using bland adjectives instead of narrative to describe her experiences at camp and in Scandinavia. With better storytelling, the essay [might] have finished with the same punch as it started.

ALYSSA SAUNDERS

As the only Jewish student in my predominantly Christian elementary school, I devoured opportunities to teach and learn about cultural and religious traditions. Every December I not only listened attentively to stories about my classmates' Christmas celebrations, but also meticulously prepared a report for my class to explain the Hanukkah story and dispel popular myths such as the Menorah Fairy. One year, when I told my teacher I had no ornaments to adorn the class's tree, he presented me with a needlepoint Star of David to fasten to the treetop. My fourth-grade sensibilities urged me to be polite, but I had a nagging, instinctive reaction that my star did not belong. In this environment, I grew up both cognizant and appreciative of difference in a largely homogeneous community.

Over time, my youthful delight in sharing holiday customs matured into an intellectual curiosity about how heritage influences thinking about societal issues. As an undergraduate at Harvard, I witnessed the majority of the student body distill itself into uniform social circles, but I refused to fall into this comfortable pattern of self-segregation. Instead, I sought a forum in which to engage with diversity. I devoted myself to *Diversity & Distinction*, a glossy black-and-white campus publication that explored the shades of grey of social issues.

As a writer for *Diversity & Distinction*, I broke the unspoken rule of self-segregation. On one occasion, an interviewee's misconceptions of me hampered and nearly terminated our discussion. In order to compose an article about the impact of the Arab-Israeli conflict on campus, I met with several students of Palestinian descent during Ramadan after the daily fast. Balancing a plate of chickpeas and rice on my lap, I began to speak when one woman noticed my Star of David necklace and interrupted me. "You're Jewish; do you have a problem with me?" she asked with suspicion, turning the tables. By completing the interview—and writing a balanced representation of the issues—I rose to the challenge of having an interethnic dialogue despite my interviewee's initial hostility toward my heritage.

Two years later, after I ascended to the position of editor-in-chief, I faced an abrupt job-interview question that gave me pause. "Why's a girl like you the editor of a magazine like that?" my interviewer asked bluntly. My identity as a white, Jewish, middle-class woman did not fit her stereotype of the editor of a diversity-oriented magazine. Several of my peers similarly probed why I labored to foster dialogue about topics perceived as "minority issues." By accepting self-segregation as the norm rather than expecting students to confront diversity, these individuals failed to understand the advantage of having diversity on campus.

If the ostensibly diverse groups featured prominently on college brochure covers do not materialize, the educational benefits of diversity are lost. A critical part of my own liberal arts education occurred during meetings with the magazine's unusually diverse staff. My fellow writers and I brought our unique upbringings and experiences to debates about disparate topics, ranging from interracial relationships to the war in Iraq. As the editor of *Diversity & Distinction*, I provided readers with a taste of this candid—and at times confrontational—discourse. By surmounting many of the prevalent ethnic, racial, and religious divisions on campus, I not only gained valuable experience in cross-cultural dialogue, but also helped to enrich the academic experience of my classmates. I am proud that *Diversity & Distinction* encouraged students to engage with one another and reap the benefits of living and learning in a diverse community.

Review by Shifra Mincer

This candidate uses a gripping anecdotal introduction to keep the admissions officer interested in the essay. The introduction serves to paint a vivid picture of the candidate, as she explains her thoughts about the Christmas tree incident with her teacher.

The introduction contextualizes the claim made in the first sentence of the second paragraph: the reader understands why diversity issues are important to Saunders. The rest of the essay is personal and detailed as it describes through anecdotes the daily work of a writer and, eventually, editor of *Diversity & Distinction*. Saunders's résumé says that she worked for the magazine, but it cannot explain the challenges and the life lessons learned from this work. The essay is the law candidate's opportunity to show the way that personal experiences have shaped his or her interests, and this essay accomplishes that goal very well. The candidate does not list what she has done as if she is rewriting her résumé, but instead describes the person behind the résumé. And in her account of an interview with an Arab woman, she includes details, such as a description of balancing her food on her lap, which add significant color to her essay.

Saunders emphasizes her strengths as an evenhanded interviewer and as a discussion leader. She is careful not to point out her weaknesses, a common mistake made by many law school applicants. However, this personal statement lacks one major component that is crucial in a law-school admissions essay—Saunders does not explain how her work with diversity issues will help her law career. She never explains why she wants to be a lawyer, or how a law degree will help her pursue her career plans. In fact, she never discusses career plans.

Finally, the conclusion does not clearly tie together the entire essay because it does not revive images from the introduction. It would have been helpful to bring the essay together by wrapping it up with references to earlier parts of the piece.

WORDS AND LANGUAGE

KATHERINE BUCHANAN

I let the words hang there for just a second, my pencil suspended over the graphite slashes: "Instead, for Ishmael, truth is constituted." The phrase I have just written dares me to leave it there. I deliberate; the pencil taps. Then spurred by some violent synapses in the brain, I smear out the last two words with the nub of my eraser. Something about the phrase nags at me. Is truth constituted? Constructed? Forged or fashioned? I try out the possibilities in a whisper, swishing the syllables slowly, waiting for their connotative finish.

Words have always possessed me like this: as a writer I am attuned to the nuances of experience I can set in motion with my language. As a reader, I delight in texts purposely crafted to disclose their complexity in response to my questioning. Given this passion on the one hand and practical necessity on the other, I have always sought out places where language influences our material reality, sites where words matter to truth. That language and reality are somehow connected, I've never doubted. After all, it's not simply that words reflect the world; it's that the world often takes its cues from words.

Built into this constitutive power of language is the assumption that through a text readers are united across time and space. My intuition further tells me that this capacity of a single *object* to bring together an infinite number of *subjects* cannot be wholly unrelated to finding collective solutions to common problems. Trying to better understand the abstract relation between text and democracy led to my interdisciplinary English major. The literature, history, and political science courses that I have taken have exposed me to an array of critical frameworks with which to investigate the truth-value of language in the specific context of twentieth-century America. Accordingly, in my honors thesis about high-school American literature textbooks, I try to make connections between multicultural literary-canon expansion—students being reflected in texts—and broader participation in a pluralistic democracy.

In the course of researching my thesis, I came to an unexpected realization: the changes I am documenting were enabled and justified almost entirely by the introduction of the word *diversity* to legal discourse. The relation between language and reality, then, is more complicated than a simple one-to-one correspondence; law mediates between signifier (word) and signified (reality) in American society. Law is the *object* that unites an infinite number of American *subjects*, governing—sometimes subtly and sometimes dramatically—our entries and roles in society. Yet for all its privileged status, law is still a collection of words, replete with benign and malignant ambiguities.

Thinking of the law as text has given me courage to challenge it. I've come to realize that the legal mediation process cannot happen without agents; law exists as a means of power only so long as we discuss and occasionally disagree over the final assignation of its signifiers. Ultimately, the force propelling me toward law as a career is the same force that drew me back to the irksome truth phrase in my paper on Herman Melville. I see my mission as similar to that of Melville's maverick narrator: questioning tradition and its reproduction of iniquity by appropriating its forms for the formerly invisible. It can only follow that for me, as for Ishmael, truth *cannot* be impersonally constituted; rather, it is dialectically articulated. It is the promise of direct and sustained engagement in this process that is the compelling reason I want to be one of the specialized agents we call attorneys.

Review by Rachel Banks

Katherine Buchanan's essay is effective because it demonstrates a sophisticated understanding of the role law plays in society, and how her studies to date make her uniquely qualified to work within that legal framework. The opening of her essay is unexpected and refreshing, and immediately introduces the theme of language that permeates the entire essay. Synthesizing both her work on a Melville paper and the admissions essay question, she artfully brings together her work in the English department with her desire to be an attorney. When she defines the legal system, she proves to the admissions officer that she has an innovative viewpoint, and that she has a mode of thinking that sets her apart from others.

If you are writing an essay about the importance of language, you better make sure that your essay reads clearly, and Buchanan's does just that. Her writing style eschews long, cumbersome words in favor of a simpler, more crisp writing style. Rather than try to impress through use of a complex vocabulary, she proves that she is knowledgeable by expressing her complicated thoughts in digestible terms.

Her essay is strong to the end, where the piece comes full circle when it responds to her initial question of how we define truth. Her reasons for wanting to be a lawyer are very clear. Buchanan has made the commonplace description of interests and talents into a distinguishing illustration of her ideas concerning the legal system.

JERILIN BUZZETTA

It might sound silly, but for most of my life I forgot I was part Chinese. With auburn hair, deep-set eyes, olive skin, and a conspicuous Italian surname, I am racially incognito. Over the years, Brazilians, Pakistanis, and even Turkic Uighurs from China's westernmost Xinjiang Province have tried to claim me as their own. Fleeting reminders of my Chinese side emerged with my expert use of chopsticks and taste for pungent thousand-year-old eggs, but still it was easy to forget. Mom wanted me to speak only perfect American English and told me to be grateful that I resembled Dad. That way, she thought, her daughter could sidestep discrimination and enter the real world unshackled by minority status.

Until I enrolled in Elementary Mandarin at [my university] on a whim of curiosity in 2002, I had a four-word Chinese vocabulary: "kiss," "sleep," "baby," and "puppy." For eighteen years, I admired my Chinese heritage from afar as an exclusive community to which, despite my genetic link, I had no access. By traveling the demanding and rewarding road from a four- to six-thousand-word vocabulary, I have evolved from an observer to a participant of Chinese culture.

I began to study written Chinese by robotically scrawling each character seventy-five times with a pencil. This crude method caused my hand to dissociate from my brain and resulted in zero recollection the next day. Today, I use a brush and ink to write each character ten times at a deliberate pace. One glance at my lopsided calligraphy would make any member of the Chinese literati cringe, but now I can compose articulate handwritten essays without a dictionary. While memorizing visual characters is difficult, learning the associated spoken tones (high, rising, dipping, falling, or neutral) makes Chinese downright sinister. To a novice who once confused the vaguely homophonic *li mao* (polite) and *liu mang* (vagabond) in public, remembering that *shí liù* means "sixteen" and *shí liú* means "pomegranate" seemed impossible. In response, I devised a method of memorizing tones by reciting words in the exaggerated style of a Beijing opera singer. I usually remember to shed the dramatic accent when I participate in weekly conversation classes. . . .

Now and then, I give myself "environment quizzes" to test my ability to name every object and action I see. "Laptop, keys, insecticide . . ."

Words and Language

Any unknown item joins my list of experiential vocabulary. Last night, I begrudgingly added "centipede" to my inventory when I saw one scuttle across my bathroom floor. For a lighthearted twist on informal practice, I translate pop songs to Mandarin. Instead of singing in the shower, I speak in Chinese. My strangest technique, exuberance training, derives from an approach by which entire stadiums of Chinese students of English shout their lessons in unison. This method is said to imbue people with confidence to speak their second language in public. The first time I shouted about "seeing a doctor" from a grassy knoll on the outskirts of campus, a public safety officer interrupted my lesson. She shot me a bewildered look when I explained my method and told me to keep it down. Now, I save exuberance training for soundproof study rooms.

Exuberance training improved my confidence in the classroom, but it did not fully prepare me for my months abroad in 2004. Within days of arriving in Beijing, I stood at the gates of the Summer Palace, twirled my umbrella like a baton while humming a tune by Fleetwood Mac, and clocked an unsuspecting elderly woman on the head. Mortified, I blurted out, "Sorry!" as a knee-jerk reaction before realizing she didn't understand English. The unlucky victim muttered "*Yang gui*" (foreign ghost) under her breath and scurried away before I could redeem myself by apologizing in Chinese. At that moment, I felt disappointed in my failure to communicate such a simple message. My ability to read sixth-grade versions of *Romance of the Three Kingdoms* and *The Art of War* meant nothing if I could not function in Chinese society.

Despite countless hours of calligraphy, tones, and grammar, I still spoke Chinese with the sluggish step of silent translation. To coach my brain to achieve the next level of fluency by thinking in Mandarin, I limited myself to a Chinese-Chinese dictionary and defined all new words in simple terms I already knew. In my mind, "owl" became "big-headed bird," and "battery" became "energy pill." My rudimentary definitions did not deviate far from the correct literal translations: "owl" is "cat-headed hawk," and "battery" is "electricity pool." Within weeks of using this method, I began to drop the step of silent translation. Upon returning to the United States, I even dreamed in Chinese. At last, my brain could function solely in Mandarin.

During four and a half months in China, I explored a socialist village; shared a banquet with local officials; interviewed prostitutes for a research paper; toured a factory that manufactured feminine hygiene products; harvested cultured pearls from an oyster farm; camped on the Great Wall; circumambulated the Jokhang temple with Tibetan Buddhists; and helped a girl catch her runaway pig. I spoke with people across China about religion, terrorism, foot-binding, plastic surgery, gender roles, and other controversial topics. Inquisitive taxi drivers who drove me between my dorm and workplace in downtown Beijing treated me as a window into U.S. society: "Why does the U.S. bully other countries?" "Why do Americans eat so much?" On my final day in Beijing, the driver who took me to the airport said, "We need people like you to make sure the U.S. and China become close friends. You will return to work in Beijing." Now that I have exhausted my university's Mandarin classes, I attempt to carry out [the driver's] prophecy by dedicating two hours a day to studying Chinese on top of my regular course load.

Back in the United States, I wondered when I would use Chinese outside my conversation classes. To my surprise, my newfound bilingualism enabled me to help thirty people escape the cold one night. As we waited in a freezing downpour on the sidewalk of Eighty-eight East Broadway for a midnight Chinatown bus from New York to D.C., the ticket seller approached my boyfriend and asked, in Chinese, if he spoke Mandarin. I interrupted with, "No, he's Korean." Her eyes lit up at the sound of my slight Beijing accent; she was relieved to find a Chinese speaker among the diverse group of travelers. She instructed me to lead the crowd to a shelter seven blocks away, where we dried off and sipped hot tea while waiting for the delayed bus. If only that poor lady I hit on the head in front of the Summer Palace could see me now.

Maybe she would realize that I am more than a good-for-nothing *yang gui* after all.

Review by A. Haven Thompson

Buzzetta opens her essay with vivid language that allows her reader to see, taste, and hear the evidence of her mixed racial heritage—her deep-set eyes, her taste in food, and even her mother's voice. And she is quick to establish the thesis of her essay: as she explains in the second paragraph, her demanding journey toward fluency in Chinese profoundly affected her understanding of herself, her heritage, and her future.

Buzzetta incorporates anecdotes and metaphors into her prose, explaining her path to linguistic proficiency in a clear and engaging manner. The essay's structure gives it an easy flow, as she sandwiches details about the mundane tasks of language learning between colorful anecdotes recounting two pivotal experiences. The first, an encounter with a Chinese woman who calls her a "foreign ghost," humbles her and incites her to study even harder. The second—about the pride she feels when her bilingualism allows her to help strangers find shelter on a cold night—demonstrates her fluency in the language, but it also highlights her compassion for the less fortunate.

The strength of Buzzetta's essay is twofold. Buzzetta establishes herself as a stylish, creative writer on the one hand; at the same time, she conveys her ability to devote herself intensively to whatever task is at hand. She uses concrete examples—such as . . . exuberance training and the "environment quizzes"—to describe her tremendous work ethic and drive. She tempers that intensity with humorous personal details (such as humming Fleetwood Mac songs to herself) that allude to her personal life and interests. She is not, after all, merely a devotee to the Chinese language.

Although Buzzetta focuses mainly on her experiences in college and in China, she cleverly uses a conversation with a Chinese cabdriver to reveal her higher aspirations: to work in Beijing and to foster understanding between the United States and China. Her artful and amusing prose expresses her determination as well as her affability.

DEREK COLLA

I have found myself in a lot of uncomfortable situations over the course of my life, but none more so than the first time I visited my Italian relatives in Parma. This visit took place in the fall of 2003 while I was spending the semester studying in Rome.

No one in my immediate family had ever met our Italian cousins, but an older American aunt who was acquainted with them sent a letter arranging for me to stay at their apartment for a weekend in early October. I thought they would probably be able to speak English, and if they did not, I hoped that the Italian I had picked up during my first month in Rome would suffice. As soon as I stepped off the train and tried to start a conversation, I realized the gross inadequacy of my Italian skills. Asking people how to get to the bus station and ordering at a restaurant are quite different from carrying on a dialogue with anxious relatives. Speaking only in situations of the former variety, I had built up a false sense of confidence that quickly washed away in Parma. My cousins were extremely gracious and hospitable (giving me so much food to eat that I nearly killed myself trying to be polite), but the experience left me disappointed because I believed the visit had the potential to be much more meaningful and enjoyable. My great-grandfather Madardo Colla emigrated in the early 1900s, and I wished to find out the circumstances behind his decision, the history of my ancestors in Italy, and information about any relatives in Italy.

Words and Language

Because of my deficient language skills, I missed the opportunity to learn these specific details about my background and develop a more robust self-identity. I agreed to come back and visit again in December, mainly because I did not know how to respectfully decline, and I consoled myself with the realization that I had another two months to improve before returning.

I felt a real lack of self-confidence after my dismal performance that weekend, but during the train ride back to Rome I convinced myself that I had the ability to learn the language over the next two months if I worked hard enough. Fervently setting about the task, I initiated conversations with anyone [who] would speak to me in Italian, and carried a pocket dictionary in order to go back and look up words I did not understand. By watching television, working through the *Gazetta dello Sport* at least a few times a week, and participating in a language course at John Cabot, I gradually improved my Italian, and on the second trip to Parma I spoke well enough to ask everything I desired to know. While not completely fluent, I possessed the ability to understand and be understood. Comfortable and engaged, I felt rewarded for the hard work I had put in to conquer a problem that had seemed overwhelming after the first visit. Just being able to say, "The food is wonderful, but if I eat any more I think I will explode," was invaluable.

I think this experience demonstrates the sort of person I am, and why I believe I will do well in law school. Some people are so brilliant and talented that they immediately succeed at nearly everything they try by relying solely upon natural ability. In high school, innate talent carried my academic performance, but the parity of ability in college forced me to work much harder. I developed the capability to learn quickly from mistakes and became resilient and persistent. This builds character in a person, and character is the most valuable asset I have gained from my time at college. As I look ahead to the challenges that law school will present, I am confident that I have the right mix of ability, work ethic, and positive attitude to thrive.

Review by Sahil K. Mahtani

What is immediately admirable about this essay is its honest acknowledgment of the writer's limitations. Colla is not a legal genius, he makes clear, but a hard worker. Correspondingly, the essay emphasizes the triumph of a determined will leading to an achievement that could not be gleaned from reading a transcript. This is good, because it adds a level of depth to the writer's application: the essay is not a mere dramatization of information already provided, but an original perspective in its own right.

The writing in the essay is not particularly decorative, but its clarity might cater to a speed-reading admissions officer. What is missing, however, is any indication as to why Colla would like to study law. There is a hint of an interest in immigration when he speaks of his long-standing curiosity in his great-grandfather's origins, but this is left unelaborated. The writer could expand this isolated historical rumination by explaining—or at least indicating—his plans for the future in light of his past experience. Doing so would convey a sense of purpose.

Still, there is much to emulate in Colla's essay. The picture one gets is that of a decent, hardworking young man with an interest in his community and unique Italian heritage. The old-school accent on "character" also fits with this image. Coupled with quiet humor throughout ("if I eat any more I think I will explode"), Colla comes across as a true gentleman with a strong desire to learn. Remember as you write your own essay, you don't necessarily need to have flowery language and portray life-altering events to have an impact; sometimes a more humble essay can do the trick.

SAMUEL KARDON

My passion for reading, writing, and analyzing literature has always been the most important component of my intellectual life. What draws me toward art with words, I have come to realize, is less the promise of insight into the human condition than a love for the process of analysis and expression. My goal as a student and worker is the construction of meaningful interpretations, and that is why I want to pursue a career as a lawyer and attend law school at Harvard University.

I love the feeling I get as I read closely, scanning for evidence that I can use to express an argument about an aspect of the intertwined bundle of symbols, images, characters, and themes that make up a good book. Creating original interpretations is its own reward, but I do not want to dedicate my life to academic pursuits. Writing an analytical paper sometimes made me feel like I was rephrasing a question, not providing an answer, even though I was striving to clarify uncertainty, creating comprehension where none existed before. I honed my ability as a critic as my education progressed, but it was not until the fall of my senior year, when I took a course in literary theory, that I knew what permanent knowledge I would take away from my studies.

I had always avoided literary theory because I didn't like the seemingly contradictory idea of making rigid rules for the open and creative process of literary interpretation, but I was wrong. Literary theory, I learned, was not meant to impose limits, but rather to describe and help one understand how and why the entire process of interpretation worked. The texts we dealt with were the most challenging I had ever encountered, and the harder I concentrated on penetrating them, the more they rewarded me. Gradually, I started to apprehend a new way to look at the problem I had always faced as an English student: the harder one tries to isolate the essence of a text, the more it resists conclusive interpretation. Analysis breaks problems of comprehension down into questions that can only be answered by posing several smaller and more exact questions which, in turn, require even more inquiry and so on and so forth. While I had come up with many interesting conclusions, I was well aware that they did not represent objective facts that might serve as the last word on even an isolated aspect of the work, no matter how rigorously proven.

Any conclusion we can draw can only be valid in a relative sense dependent on its context, but this limitation is also what allows and compels us to continue investigating, only in a different direction. Instead of building theories outwardly in a linear manner, striving to reach the alluringly distant horizon of complete understanding, we must travel back inward toward the source, questioning what has already been accepted by describing it in more detail, until a functional way to move forward becomes apparent. This is the core of how analysis works, in any discipline, and it was studying literary theory and majoring in English that taught me how to apply it. That ability, combined with the success and satisfaction I derive from exercising it, are the primary reasons I think I will be an excellent law student and, eventually, an excellent lawyer.

Even though laws are generally enacted with explicit purposes in mind, circumstances shift and change necessitating new interpretations. Law, like literature, is a series of texts that can be easily misunderstood if not read carefully. Both the lawyer and the literary critic aspire to conduct analysis with precision, insight, and the dispassionate conviction not to accept convention without careful consideration; however, the literary critic's analysis, if it is done correctly, only raises more questions. The entire legal system is based on the principle that laws can be written in language that is clear and comprehensive enough to resolve disputes and provide appropriate regulation. Practicing law solves real problems, helping social entities, from individuals to corporations to governments, function better and understand their limits and potentialities more clearly. I hope to do this work myself someday, but first I want to learn about the theory and language of law in an intellectually charged environment like Harvard

Law School. I look forward to sharing this pursuit of understanding with classmates who can shift and challenge my perspectives as I can shift and challenge theirs.

Review by Dina Guzovsky

Samuel's essay is impressive for how much ground it covers in so little space: he tells us a lot about himself while also giving an original answer to the question of why he wants to be a lawyer. He loves analyzing texts, but is sometimes frustrated that he's just "rephrasing a question, not providing an answer." Thus, he'll love the law, where he can combine his passion for analysis with his desire to solve "real problems, help social entities."

Samuel's essay is also strong because he makes it clear that he is speaking about something he loves and is passionate about. His use of specific detail instead of vague generality helps bring his love of analysis home to the reader. For example, Samuel starts the second paragraph with a particularly strong, specific sentence: "I love the feeling I get as I read closely, scanning for evidence that I can use to express an argument . . ." The reader feels he is right there as Samuel sits hunched over his desk, underlining furiously. Samuel also plays to his own academic strengths by speaking intelligently about complicated questions of literary analysis. Stylistically, Samuel shines. The transition sentences between paragraphs are especially elegant, and his words are carefully chosen—it's clear Samuel spent a lot of time honing his essay.

If Samuel's essay has a weakness, it's the middle chunk. The section about his literary theory class seems parenthetical to the main topic at hand—he delves a little too deeply into specific issues of textual interpretation without introducing anything new about himself that wasn't already explained in the first few paragraphs. Nevertheless, this is on the whole a passionate and original essay, one which showcases both Samuel's academic passions and his interest in the law.

PAIGE MESSEC

My first car, you could say, was a vehicle for self-expression. I was seventeen, and it was a white 1992 Nissan Sentra, an androgynous-looking car that I named Andy. Most seventeen-year-olds have an exaggerated sense of connection between their cars and their identities, and I was no exception. To my father's dismay, within weeks of purchasing the car, I had plastered the entire rear end with bumper stickers.

Although I like to think I've changed and grown since then, the only sticker I no longer agree with is the one that said, "If it's too loud, you're too old." The rest are still reflections of what I stand for. Take, for example, the one that said, "Eschew obfuscation." You might think it's a joke, which it is, but it's also a statement of the value I place on good, clear writing. Actually, I have a passion for grammar and even have a favorite punctuation mark (the semicolon). I can quote passages from *The Elements of Style*. I can't read without editing, mentally striking out unnecessary words and rearranging phrases. One of the most important talents that a person in any field can possess is the ability to make complex ideas understandable, and this requires straightforward and succinct writing. This ability is especially necessary in law, where there is an unfortunate prevalence of words like "hitherto" and "aforementioned."

The sticker that read, "Those who ignore nature are bound to deplete it" . . . expressed my commitment to environmental issues. My experience working at the Pew Center on Global Climate Change for the last year has solidified that commitment; perhaps more important, the serious and professional attitude of the Pew Center has shown me the kind of approach I want to take toward environmental issues. Environmentalists often have problems relating to other people whose primary concern is not the environment, and this impedes the success of the movement. To be taken seriously, environmentalists need to move away from their image as a bunch of technophobic, econophobic tree-huggers with pink hair and facial piercings. Law will allow me to take the kind of practical, professional approach that the movement often lacks. The movement needs people who understand environmental laws, who can make them understandable to the public, and who will work to improve them. Taking my strengths into account, [law] is the career that will offer me the best opportunities to effect changes in the field.

Women's issues is another area in which law would allow me to take a pragmatic approach. Feminism has gotten a bad reputation. I first realized this when the sticker "Feminism is the radical notion that women are people" was torn off my car. The first time it happened, I called my bumper-sticker company to order a replacement. They sent me three extras, in case it disappeared again. Every time somebody ripped it off, I put another one back on. I wasn't going to let the unpopularity of the movement discourage me. When I got to college, I tried to join the campus feminist magazine. The staff, however, decided that our first feature article should be on the history of the vibrator, and I couldn't see how that was going to win over any of the undecideds. I have always preferred a constructive approach to one that merely draws attention. Articles like that will "empower" a small percentage of people, but it will alienate the rest. To make progress, we need to dedicate ourselves to serious issues that affect women. Not only that, but we need people who are positioned to make changes. Among other things, women's causes can use good advocates in the law.

I wrecked the car two days before I was to leave for college, and we had to sell it to a salvager. Though I was dismayed at the time, it strikes me now that the crash marks an important change for me. High school is a time for figuring out what you think of the world and announcing it. In college and at work, I shifted from identifying and proclaiming to doing. I hope law school and beyond will be a time for more development and more action. Because after all, as my favorite bumper sticker says, "Actions speak louder than bumper stickers."

Review by Lois E. Beckett

Paige describes the bumper stickers on her first car to showcase her different interests and abilities. It's a gimmick, but she pulls it off through careful organization and vivid writing.

Personal essays need to have the same well-thought-out structure as an academic paper. In a twist on the old five-paragraph essay, Paige chooses five bumper stickers: an introduction, a conclusion, and three topic stickers to explore her interests in writing, the environment, and feminism. She ties each of these topics into her desire to be a lawyer. By themselves, Paige's reasons for becoming a lawyer are not groundbreaking, but each of the sections benefits from her use of details. By including particulars like the make, year, and name of her car, Paige's essay strikes a balance between generalizing, which might bore admissions officers, and offering extraneous information. The trick is to choose relevant details: try to say what is important in the most specific way possible.

Paige includes the anecdote about the feminist bumper stickers getting ripped off her car four times not only because it's a funny story, but because it demonstrates the cultural backlash against feminism. Telling that story is much more effective than stating that she perceives feminism to be unpopular today in many places.

In part, Paige's essay succeeds simply because she's a good writer. But even if your prose is not naturally as polished as hers, you can use some of her techniques. Choose vivid verbs, like "plastered," rather than weighing down your piece with adjectives. Vary your sentence structure by alternating short and long sentences and dependent and independent clauses. If you have four sentences in a row that start with "I" or "Then I" or "Since I," that's a problem. And, of course, as Paige suggests, avoid "afore-mentioned" and other legalese.

Paige also finds the right note to end on. "Actions speak louder than bumper stickers" brings the essay to a tidy close, but it also allows her to poke fun at the essay and show the admissions committee she has not been caught up in her own gimmick.

DAVID WERTIME

I joined the Peace Corps prepared for a great challenge, but life in Fuling came at me in small bedeviling pieces: steep, crooked warrens; a swirl of grit and fog that enveloped the city; stifled laughs and tiny prejudices. I didn't mind living alone, and living simply. But without the companionship of Chinese I felt like a child, my world a blur of perplexing events and mysterious ciphers. Too proud to remain an ignorant spectator, I retreated to my apartment for hours each day and began teaching myself to read.

Chinese characters proved an apt partner for eager study: orderly, elegant, responsive to my advances. The intimidating tangles of lines dissolved obediently before methodical inquiry: "big" became a man holding his arms out, "show" became a sacrificial altar with a goblet resting on its surface. In my dreams I manipulated these characters at will, inventing new ones that glowed big and bright like neon lights. Giddy with new knowledge, I read menus and street signs aloud to anyone who would listen.

After several months menus gave way to newspaper articles, and I rejoiced to find Chinese a language of austere precision. Whether simple or esoteric, sentences ran in digital chains free of articles, tenses, or verb conjugations. Where English words had seemed to mask their origin, Chinese shone pure and visceral: "vigorous," for example, consisted of "fire" and "explosion" side by side. The most banal sentences swam with challenges, but I could always reduce them to a form solid and unassailable.

Although substantial on paper, characters collapsed together as they passed into the reality of everyday speech. Even the careful tones and sturdy sibilance of proper Mandarin resembled a jumble of like sounds and accidental rhymes. In the local tongue, that fragile structure dissolved, flipping tones upside down, drowning whole phonemes. With every loud, lightning-fast sentence, the language I had so fervently sought seemed to turn its back on me. Feeling thwarted, I referred to the dialect as the locals did: "*tu hua,*" or "dirt speak." Only through my friendships did I begin to see the dialect as a window into a unique culture, not an indictment of my intelligence. My Mandarin met with praise, but "*tu hua*" met with warmth. For a year my friends patiently spoke a language taught to them by bureaucrats; as this became less necessary, they became more themselves. They laughed easily and gleefully taught me the lush range of local insults, including my favorite, "Your mother sells bean sprouts!" Even such simple phrases proved surprisingly potent to hurt or console. I realized I wasn't learning a dialect; I was learning Fuling's first language.

Through this language, I began to see the real characters around me almost as clearly as the written characters I had first engaged. Wry and sarcastic, my friends correctly described both their dialect and themselves as "vigorous." *H*s left the mouth as *F*s because, legend had it, people there used to blow so hard when they spoke that the sounds slowly became indistinguishable. Emotion poured out in the exaggerated tonality of every sentence, free of the fetters of Mandarin's refined inflection. Even age became irrelevant in a vernacular both brutal and endearing—Fuling boys were "babies," the men "whelps."

As I have embraced the ambiguity and uncertainty of Chinese, it has finally begun to assume the clarity I once sought in the strictures of a grammar book. Paradoxically, the more I devote myself to this search, the less I live or die with success or failure. Chinese itself becomes a metaphor for the joy of language—that greatest of collective enterprises, inseparable from human beings or their cultures, as vexing and as lovely as both.

Review by William C. Marra

This essay's success lies in its ability to convey the author's personal growth with a minimum amount of explicit introspection. Notice that but for its final sentence, the essay follows the author as he looks *outward* at the Chinese characters before him. Thanks to the author's use of rich and descriptive adjectives, we effortlessly track his increasingly intimate relationship with a novel language. The whole exercise provides a window into the author's cultural assimilation, his open-mindedness and ability to learn about new cultures and concepts—all without any explicit statement that this is going on.

When writing your essay, keep in mind the importance of showing rather than telling, as demonstrated in this essay. Wertime does not simply tell us that Chinese characters are all unique; he provides concrete examples of shapes and sounds evinced by the characters. Similarly, the author does not tell us that his knowledge of language has improved his connection with society; he shows it using examples of him interacting with others through language.

The one part of the essay that could use improvement is the conclusion, which is not ambitious enough. Wertime does not extend beyond the reach of language to draw any broader lesson for life. His conclusion is that "Chinese itself becomes a metaphor for the joy of language." The statement is unconvincing—Chinese *is* a language, and the logic seems circular. This is not to say that your conclusion needs to make some unique revelation about the purpose of life. You should, however, try to extend beyond the scope of your essay and draw lessons for other areas of life. If your essay is about language, make sure the payoff is more than simply that you learned the value of language. The same goes for sports, movies, or any other topic you choose.

"I WANT TO BE A LAWYER BECAUSE . . ."

REBECCA BAZAN

I am left-handed, but I cannot cut with left-handed scissors. My elementary-school teachers encouraged me with special lefties, but alas I could not make them work. I would awkwardly grasp them and try to cut, but succeeded only in bending the paper and the scissors. Finally, I realized that unlike most people I write with my left hand, but like most people I needed right-handed scissors. This is, in short, the story of my life.

At first glance my red hair and fair skin lead people to deduce that I am Irish, but just like my handedness, appearances only tell half the story. My mother's ancestors are from Ireland, while my father's are from Mexico. I enjoy my grandmother's fideo, a traditional Mexican soup, just as much as I enjoy my other grandmother's Irish soda bread. I grew up playing Irish dolls and Spanish bingo, but never did I feel trapped between the two worlds; they are conjoining pieces of my heritage.

Perhaps that is why as a child I reveled in fitting puzzle pieces together to create a complete picture. I have always enjoyed problem solving, especially working complex math equations down to a simple, elegant solution. I now know that although being able to solve problems succinctly is a great skill, not everything fits so easily into one neat box, myself included. I am a lefty who cannot use left-handed scissors; I have light skin but my father's first language is Spanish; I am a political science major who loves math. Realizing that I cannot be contained in one category has helped me enjoy the order in things while appreciating that which defies simple classification.

The summer after my junior year of high school I worked for an attorney who specializes in child support collection. Part of my job was to create a client database so he could easily access all the pertinent information for each client's case. This assignment was a perfect challenge because it allowed me to utilize my passion for puzzles and to be sensitive to the details of each case. One day my employer invited me to the courthouse to watch him in action and meet local attorneys and judges. Law school was on the horizon and I knew this would be an amazing opportunity, but once we got to the courthouse I realized there were more important things to do that day. A client whose case was to go before the judge was beside herself with fear that her ex-husband would show up for court. I explained to her that he was in another state and would not come to challenge the judgment, but her history of abuse would not allow her to believe it. I decided to remain with her instead of shadowing my boss in order to keep her mind off her fear by making casual conversation. That day did not neatly conform to my plan for it, but I was glad to know that when it really mattered, I put aside my personal agenda and was of use to someone who needed me. Working in the law office that summer taught me about the legal process, teamwork in an office environment, and how to trust both my skills and my judgment of priorities.

This past summer I was honored to take part in the International Mission on Diplomacy program in Australia. Along with forty other college students, I visited Canberra, Sydney, and Cairns. We toured government buildings, met public officials, and heard lectures by aboriginal speakers. Learning the rules of Australia's electoral system was interesting, but contemplating how to work within the framework of rules to make positive changes is what really tickled my brain. This eye-opening experience cemented my desire to attend law school and enter the legal profession.

Being a lefty in a right-handed world has given me a unique perspective that allows me to appreciate both sides of an issue. I want to be involved in a profession which highlights my appreciation for structure while giving me an opportunity to utilize my creativity. The order required to practice law appeals to my appetite for problem solving, and providing people with the agency to make changes in their lives appeals to my sense of compassion. My personality and my life experiences have convinced me of my fit for law school and the legal profession.

Review by Melissa Quino McCreery

Bazan uses her left-handed theme adeptly: she introduces it with a colorful but succinct anecdote and then lets it guide the rest of her essay without overpowering it. By taking a seemingly inconsequential fact of life and transforming it into a fresh and lively story, Bazan sets herself apart from the pack as she explains why she is good at "thinking outside the box" (without ever having to resort to that trite phrase).

Once she starts talking about her work experience, Bazan has no hesitation about temporarily abandoning the metaphor rather than awkwardly forcing it to fit. This way, when she brings it back for the conclusion, the essay comes full circle and feels complete. The effect would be lost if every paragraph were plagued with the same imagery.

When she discusses her internships, Bazan highlights what she got out of her experience rather than dramatizing the importance of her work and its impact on society. She at no point asks her reader to be impressed—she lets the stories speak for themselves. This not only keeps her from sounding self-important, but results in an essay that is more engaging and personal as a result.

Nowhere in the essay does she say, "I want to be a lawyer because . . . ," or "I know I am qualified because . . . ," yet by the end her reader can finish those sentences for her, and enjoy a lighthearted story about left-handedness as a bonus.

STANLEY CHANG

A cheesy, badly acted, low-budget teen soap opera from Taiwan called *Meteor Garden* starring F4—a clique of four long-haired male models—was my summer "reading" project this year. Over the last three years, from Bangkok to Beijing, all of Southeast Asia succumbed to F4 frenzy. By the time I sat down to watch *Meteor Garden*, the boys of F4 had already filmed a sequel, released four albums, endorsed products like Pepsi and Yamaha, and temporarily retired. In F4 are lessons on pop careers brilliantly managed. Their success is a reminder of the invincible power of pop culture—a power I want to help harness as a music lawyer.

The success of *Meteor Garden* and F4 was the carefully planned work of professionals. To start with, F4's good looks and charm appealed to females. They shared a bond of loyal friendship appealing to males. They easily transitioned their on-screen personalities into musical styles. In addition, most songs on F4 albums are credited to one member, establishing each as a solo star from day one. But more importantly, F4 was able to dominate the media by focusing with laserlike precision on one sector at a time—first TV, then music, then photo books, then live concerts. They produced products maximizing the potential of each medium, raising the standard for a pop act in each instance. By conquering each medium in advancing the F4 brand, the managers have revolutionized the possibilities and scope of pop-culture marketing.

Those innovations and the infinite possibilities of those to come are the reasons I want to become a music lawyer. After having read the definitive books on music law this summer (by Passman and by Krasilovsky and Gross), I have come to understand the delicacy, even the Euclidean beauty, of a well-negotiated music contract. Lawyers in music are particularly influential because they often act like agents, guiding an artist to the proper record-label channels and building relationships with both creative and business staff. In music, as in few other fields, the lawyer directly influences the client's career directions. With years observing the U.S., U.K., and Asian pop-culture industries, as an aficionado, as General Manager of the campus radio station, and as a censor at ABC TV this summer, I feel ready to start applying and translating what I have learned to the market.

F4 has succeeded spectacularly, but they are an exception in an industry in crisis. Some have even advised me not to go into music in this economic climate. On the contrary, I see this time as the most interesting period to enter the industry, because it is today's pioneers who are abandoning decades-old thinking and establishing the revolutionary models and strategies of the next generation. A weak market favors bold action, creative thinking, and risk taking—all approaches I am eager to bring to the pop-culture industry. As F4 demonstrates, the rewards are enormous. Good music lawyers are particularly needed now because the undeveloped body of law regarding new technologies is at least partly to blame for the free fall of the industry. Lawyers must therefore be at the forefront of reshaping the industry.

Reviving the pop-culture industry is much more than a business concern, however. Five years ago, Chinatowns in Indonesia were burned and looted; today young Indonesians learn the latest Chinese songs of F4 by heart. Pop is arguably the world's most powerful force among young people, one that unites people across every barrier of language, culture, national border, or socioeconomic status. A phenomenon like *Meteor Garden* literally defines the dreams of millions. I firmly believe that there is no better way to influence and develop the potential of youth than with pop culture, and I want to be a part of that process as an entertainment lawyer.

Review by May Habib

This is an excellent piece. From the beginning, the applicant captures the reader's interest with a quick and vivid sketch of an unfamiliar Taiwanese pop music group. Stanley aspires to a career that is atypical for Harvard lawyers, so he takes the time to tell us about the music industry and what a lawyer could contribute to the field. He demonstrates knowledge about the state of the industry and acknowledges that he will have to overcome some obstacles in order to succeed. He also gives his views on where music law is undeveloped and how he plans to address those aspects. By the end of the essay, the reader is led to believe in the writer's passion for the convergence of music and law.

But though Stanley is very convincing in explaining his views on the global importance of pop culture, some of the language in the essay could have been toned down. How can a music contract have "Euclidean beauty"? And how does *Meteor Garden* "literally" define the dreams of millions? The essay could have used another read-through to tighten and clarify some sentences. Also, an additional sentence or two of background information about the author could have helped his personality come alive to a reader. The reader is left with questions, such as how his experiences at ABC as a censor shaped his career plans, or what the roots of his pop-culture obsession are.

Overall, however, the applicant distinguishes himself successfully in this essay by illustrating to the reader his unique reasons for wanting to study law.

NOELLE CHUNG

I grew up in a small town in Eastern Washington. As a preteen making the social rounds in junior high, I began supplementing my academic diet with classes at three local colleges. By the time I was thirteen, I had garnered enough credits to earn an associate-of-arts honors degree with a 4.0 GPA from Walla Walla Community College. I was nominated for student speaker at graduation. But the school's nominating committee, fearing that my exceptionally young age would upset the "traditional" student population, rescinded that nomination.

Though I realized that my relative youth and inexperience might continue to cause many such setbacks, I decided to use this situation to my advantage. I put off graduation to spend another year exploring all the disciplines the school had to offer. I also campaigned for the seat of associated student body president, declaring that my age made me no less capable of fulfilling the duties of the office. To everyone's surprise, I won the election. I then went on to serve the five thousand-plus student body in a position of leadership that allowed me to contribute to the school community on a scale I could not have achieved otherwise.

With all the transferable college credits I had compiled, I could easily have kept to the fast track through a four-year institution. Instead I adhered to my intention of exploring my academic journey to the fullest. I wiped the slate clean and entered Whitman College as a freshman after accepting its generous full-ride academic scholarship. I was determined to diversify my store of knowledge and experiences. While at Whitman, though still much younger than others, I was fortunate to participate fully in all facets of college life: living in the French language–interest house, performing with the Whitman Dance Theater troupe, swimming on our NCAA Division III team, and trying to improve the campus by serving on the Student Life Board and working as an intern for the Intercultural Center—all while making sure to continue to excel academically within the liberal arts spectrum.

My intellectual pursuits eventually culminated in the creation of a personally designed major intended to fill a gap in the Whitman curriculum revealed by the rising importance of the European Union. I successfully argued to the Board of Review that my proposed comprehensive course of interdisciplinary study would create an understanding of the increased importance of shared European culture in defining European nations. By the end of my junior year I had met all the requirements for my B.A. degree in continental European cultural studies. But once again, in the spirit of delving as deeply as possible into the resources available to me, I did not forgo my senior year.

Rather, I devoted the next eleven months to approaching my proposed disciplines from the European perspective of Paris. Living in Paris and familiarizing myself with the city's institutions, such as the Sorbonne, and its cosmopolitan organizations, such as the Société des Amis du Louvre, enhanced my ability to comprehend the daily experience of the new Europe, where I completed an eighty-page honors thesis, "A Historical and Literary Analysis of French Antisemitism between the Wars."

The summer following my junior year, Whitman presented me with the Best Summer Internship Project Award, which would fully fund my internship as a research assistant at the headquarters of the Hudson Institute. While I was working at this internationally oriented think tank, the South Korean government commissioned a report concerning the possible effects of Western free-trade agreements on Korean trade and investment. I was in charge of compiling an extensive annotated literature review. It was through this process that I first glimpsed how my undergraduate training in European affairs and the cultural sensitivity stemming from my Korean roots could both serve to facilitate a flow of knowledge between East and West in the evolving global community.

Studying abroad during my senior year confirmed my resolve to continue upon a multidisciplinary and international path that, after graduation, immediately led me to pursue a master's degree in international studies at Yonsei University's Graduate School of International Studies in Seoul, South Korea. At Yonsei's GSIS, which awarded me a full-ride academic scholarship, I have been supplementing knowledge in the history and culture of Asia and Europe with the basic disciplines of international relations, skills of methodology, and principles of economic analysis. Even here, French and Korean lines cross, specifically at the Research Institute of Comparative History and

"I Want to Be a Lawyer Because..."

Culture where, as an assistant researcher, I analyze the two countries' respective periods of mid-twentieth-century political and cultural collaboration.

I have deliberately prolonged my intellectual and social journey until now, when I am finally on the same footing, agewise, as most fresh-from-college law school applicants. I have anticipated this milestone for many years, and everything I've learned and attempted so far has been in preparation for the legal education that I consider my true academic gateway into a purposeful and self-fulfilling career. I hope, through the legal training offered by your institution, to specialize eventually in the world of international law encompassing both the Eastern and Western spheres in an era that will undoubtedly experience numerous confrontations of global proportions.

Review by April Yee

Chung's achievements are extraordinary, and any reader would enjoy reading an in-depth account of any one of them. But Chung painstakingly unearths the contents of her curriculum vitae in a space that she could have used to delve into any one of the impressive feats she lists, such as her nomination for college class speaker at the age of thirteen, her advanced studies in Paris, or how she has explored her Korean roots in Seoul. This is one of the few chances an admissions officer has to meet Noelle Chung the person rather than Noelle Chung the academic.

Sure, the reader is impressed by her accomplishments. But Chung's impersonal approach leaves the reader wondering if she's human. Like many writers, she falls into the trap of using too many adverbs and long words—such as "encompassing" and "supplementing"—when she could write in a more direct, personable style.

Moreover, this essay could have gone to any one of a hundred law schools. She writes that she wants to use "the legal training offered by your institution," but fails to mention Harvard's name. Stressing that she wants to go to Harvard, and only Harvard, could only flatter her readers' egos.

Though Chung's essay fails to give her reader more than an overview of her résumé, she does smartly address her "relative youth and inexperience." Identifying a weakness and showing how she has surmounted it can make readers feel Chung is ready for Harvard Law.

HAROLD DROZDOWSKI

I was five when I fought my first battle, leaping from couch to couch with a sword and shield slaying evil dragons and returning to my castle heralded by the clarion call of bugles. Sixteen years later I'm still locked in an epic struggle against the chimeras and dragons of our time, enemies that no longer breathe fire or rend with fierce claws, but kill with engineered biological weapons and improvised explosive devices. Swords and shields made out of brooms and garbage-can lids don't cut it anymore, nor do knives, guns, or bombs. The battles I fight now are won with codes and ciphers, esoteric words, and foreign languages.

For four months I was fortunate enough to be selected to work with the National Security Agency as a full-time summer hire, along with the best and brightest young minds our nation has to offer. I hold a security clearance above the top-secret level and will continue to do so for another five years. I have also been invited to continue my employment when my education comes to a close. Due to classification, I am unfortunately unable to discuss the specifics of my role in the agency, but I am able to say that, among a myriad of other skills, I garnered a knowledge and understanding of the culture of the Middle East and a strong proficiency in Modern Standard Arabic.

"I Want to Be a Lawyer Because . . ."

I declined immediate employment because I felt that I needed a law school education to reach my full potential as a government employee. I witnessed firsthand the difficulties inherent in global law enforcement and the dire need our country has for U.S. citizens fluent in Middle Eastern languages, skilled in various legal fields, and sympathetic to the dynamic *zeitgeist* in [the Middle East]. On numerous occasions I met with top-level Pentagon policy makers to discuss the state of affairs of U.S. intelligence[, and] I frequently heard the need for effective young ambassadors and diplomats whose work would preclude the need for violent intervention in foreign countries. Currently many of our representatives in these foreign countries are not only unable to fully speak the native language, but are also ignorant of various crucial social taboos and *faux pas*. As a brief example, watch the next televised meeting of U.S. officials and Middle Eastern leaders and you will inevitably see the U.S. officials sitting with one leg crossed at a right angle, as is the fashion here in the States. Unfortunately, many of our envoys are unaware that showing the bottom of the shoe in many Middle Eastern cultures is an insult akin to cursing or spitting.

Harvard Law School is certainly an institution that would prepare me for my chosen career in government service. The Islamic Legal Studies Program at HLS is one of the preeminent programs of its kind, and I'm certain that my background in intelligence would bring a unique perspective to the program. Further, the chance to contribute to a student-edited international law journal that is as well respected in the field as the *Harvard International Law Journal* is an opportunity that I would relish. A final factor in my decision to apply to HLS is something Dean Kagan wrote recently, "[T]he study of law is not an arid intellectual exercise. The study of law matters." This philosophy parallels my own in that I want to attend law school not to become a lawyer, but to study the law.

Review by Dina Guzovsky

Harold's dynamic essay is exciting to read because he has focused on a very specific interest (diplomacy) and a very precise reason he wants to study the law. His refreshingly direct style and interesting vocabulary will stand out among essays where the applicant talks about a vague love for and interest in the law but does not deal in the sort of specifics that Harold offers. From the start, the essay grabs us with the vivid image of the five-year-old Harold slaying dragons on his couch, and the parallel between that and Harold's later work for the NSA is original and effective. His mention of his top-level security clearance and work with the "best and brightest young minds" is potentially off-putting, but he's better off for mentioning them. When writing your own essay, don't be shy to mention your accomplishments, so long as you are not arrogant about them.

The essay's only weakness is that Harold does not spend enough time elaborating on how he plans to use his legal knowledge as he pursues his career in diplomacy. Space he devotes to the interesting but ultimately irrelevant fact that many diplomats don't understand social taboos could have been better used explaining how he would use a legal education in the field. This would give a better sense of what Harold wants out of law school, as well as illustrate to the admissions team that he's really thought through his decision to apply. Still, Harold's essay radiates with intelligence, ambition, and passion, and his interest in the law is clear and well articulated.

STEVE J. HOROWITZ

At thirteen—with baggy jeans and a voice that refused to change—I had my first trumpet lesson. My playing was strong, but my interest was lacking. Toward the end of that first lesson, my teacher changed the way I thought about music. I had played through De Gouy's "Bolero" for him, proud to have hit every note.

"Nice," he said, "but I've heard it before. Next week, I want you to play it your way." With that, he added my name to the score: "edited by Steve." And I began to make music.

From then until I was nineteen, music became my primary focus. Nowhere else did I feel as though I were creating meaning rather than merely receiving it. I excelled on my instrument, eventually playing at both Carnegie Hall and Lincoln Center.

Soon after I arrived at college, I began to create meaning without an instrument in hand. My first opportunity was a class on ethical theory. Instead of merely reading texts, we explored their limits. I even wrote a paper on the failure of Homeric maxims under Kant's categorical imperative. "Homeric maxims" are, naturally, rules for living according to Homer J. Simpson—my interest in ancient Greek came later. While my work at that time might have been less than groundbreaking, I was enraptured by the chance to develop my own perspective.

My interests in philosophy and music collided when I reflected, as a sophomore, on the question of peer-to-peer file sharing. I had been using file-sharing applications for years, but with mounting litigation against such services and increased attention on the criminality of copyright infringement, I decided to put my philosophical tools to work on the ethics of file sharing. But the initial search was aporetic: I needed to explore the underlying copyright theory.

The research that followed culminated in an article entitled "Rethinking Lockean Copyright and Fair Use," which was published in the *Deakin Law Review*. For the first time, my philosophical voice enjoyed a public performance. Though I did not thank my trumpet teacher, my article feels a bit like Lockean property theory, "edited by Steve." I still love music, but what is even more exciting about making music in the scholarly realm is that my voice could change the way people live their lives. I do not expect that out of "Rethinking Lockean Copyright," of course. At this point, I would be thrilled if just a few people were to read the article. But being heard has inspired me to work harder: I hope to make more noise soon.

My goal is to help shape the way society understands, regulates, and recognizes intellectual property in a digital world. I have developed a strong background already by working with David Post at Temple Law School, attending iLaw at the Berkman Center, and publishing an article on copyright. I can find no better place to continue my studies than at Harvard Law School for three reasons. First, I greatly admire Professor [William] Fisher's work, particularly the alternative compensation system he advances in *Promises to Keep*. Second, my experience at iLaw was an amazing one, and I would love to contribute in any way possible to the Berkman Center's cutting-edge research. Finally, Professor [Jonathan] Zittrain's current research on the potentially grim future of the Internet has been the primary inspiration for my current project, "Running Headlong to Our Chains: The End of the Cyberstate of Nature."

At twenty-one, my jeans are not as baggy as they once were, and my voice has settled down. But my interest in creating meaning has not subsided. I make music every day by rethinking property rights in intellectual products, by reinterpreting Kant, and of course, by playing even that old "Bolero" my own way. As a student of philosophy interested in music and law, shaping media policy is the perfect way to fuse my passions into a symphony of creativity. The laws of yesterday are not fit for the technologies of tomorrow. My goal is not to change the world, but to help resolve this discord. Perhaps one day a small part of the way the world understands and regulates intellectual property in cyberspace will be "edited by Steve."

"I Want to Be a Lawyer Because..."

Review by Bari M. Schwartz

Though at first it may seem as if Horowitz is straining to find a metaphor, the way he ultimately connects philosophy and law to his passion for music comes across as genuine as well as unique. In this way, he successfully convinces the readers how past pursuits relate to his desire to study law. The essay also draws strength from Horowitz's subtle showcasing of his awareness of current issues and evidence of the path he wants to follow upon matriculation.

The weaknesses of the essay are both stylistic and content-based. For one, many of the words seem out of place; with the tone of Horowitz's essay as conversational, words like "enraptured" are unnatural. Secondly, the bottom half of the essay reads like a résumé, and with the accompanying application, many of the accomplishments he discusses may come across as redundant. The essay is designed to bolster the reader's opinion of the applicant and add more depth to the portfolio, not repeat it ad nauseam.

Overall the essay does not stand out among a pool of other essays. While the topic is personal, by the end of the essay the writing is slightly forgettable. Though he made an attempt to boost the essay with the "edited by Steve" theme, it could have been better reinforced. Lastly, Horowitz writes about his numerous opportunities to study law, and it is not clear why Harvard is his top choice rather than just another notch on his academic belt.

BEN MAXYMUK

Everybody has always agreed that I am an exceptionally capable and intelligent person. However, over the last several years, "everybody" has been getting anxious, wondering why this kid they always said could do (or be) anything he wanted has spent much of his seven years since college bartending, temping, and wandering around the world. Actually, there were times I wondered these things myself. Although I was not nearly as unambitious as some may have thought, and I accomplished a great deal during those years, essentially everybody was right. I *was* wandering—the result of having lost my map in 1994, the summer before my senior year at Duke, when I was diagnosed with testicular cancer. After spending my first twenty-one years striving more or less uncritically for the things I was expected to want, facing mortality at such an early age changed my mind-set about the future and made it difficult, for a time, to make long-term plans. I needed time to form my own values and decide how to live my own life. Looking back, I wouldn't change anything. I know that I am now both a more complete person and a better candidate for law school than I would have been otherwise.

After the surgery at Duke Medical Center that cured my cancer, I underwent radiation therapy that lasted into the second week of my senior year. Although the physical exhaustion passed by October, the psychological and emotional adjustments took much longer. As I emerged from my initial anger and confusion, I was stripped of the sense of entitlement and possibility I had taken for granted as a Duke student. My sense of displacement deepened that winter when my parents separated after twenty-seven years. From that time on, I was both more carefree and more serious, less worried about other people's expectations and more concerned with learning about the world outside the academic bubble. Most of all, I felt a desire for stability. So while my friends left Durham to conquer the worlds of finance, medicine, and academia, I stayed behind and put down roots on the "town" side of the town-and-gown divide, and made lifelong friends there. I learned that I love food and that I am a natural cook. I started a community garden on an empty lot next to my house and got involved in the movement against the death penalty, traveling around North Carolina to participate in protests, vigils, conferences, and meetings. And gradually, I realized that I found meaning in life through concern for my friends and for the equity and welfare of my community. Following some months traveling and studying Spanish in Ecuador and the Galápagos, I serendipitously found a job I loved at Duke. Although I began as an inexpert temporary employee, the return to an academic environment and the challenge of mastering a new discipline stirred my initiative; I was promoted over the span of sixteen months to Web designer and then team leader of the school's Web development group.

After a time, I realized that the two or three years I planned to spend in Durham had turned into seven, that I had learned what I had stayed to find out, and that I was ready to move on. As an undergraduate, I chose to major in English because of a love of rhetorical analysis and close textual reading; later, what I found compelling about computers and computer languages was the analytical rigor and technical minutiae. Managing technical projects and tweaking HTML code provided day-to-day tests in design and logic, and I enjoyed the challenge of teaching and making technical material understandable to laypeople. However, the work lacked the depth of critical thought and the political and social engagement I am seeking in a career. I want to create a professional role that fully engages me intellectually and directly reflects my values and my concern for social justice. While there are a number of ways I might accomplish this, the law is the one best matched to my skills and interests. Today I feel prepared and excited to apply my experiences and strengths to the law. And because of the time I took to ground myself and develop as a person over the last seven years, I know I can be an excellent classmate, an active member of the law school and civic community, and ultimately a better advocate and scholar.

Review by Nicholas K. Tabor

Maxymuk delves into some very personal issues and feelings in his admissions essay—and it's a gamble. A cancer diagnosis and the separation of one's parents are heady events that can play heavily into a person's career motivations; however, it's difficult to discuss emotional issues in such a short essay without losing the focus of the piece. Maxymuk balances these concerns tremendously well, conveying the significance of the personal events, yet only insofar as they led to his applying to law school. His essay demonstrates that if you're going to write about deeply personal issues, be honest and up front about them, and focus on them throughout. Through the essay, Maxymuk indicates many personal characteristics that befit an HLS applicant—a taste for academia, a "love of rhetorical analysis and close textual reading," and a tack for "critical thought"—which might not shine through in the rest of his application. He's telling a story, one that's both compelling and to the point.

However, Maxymuk's mistake is his lede. It conveys a sense of perfection and personal infallibility; he does well in the remainder of the essay to show he's still learning about himself and gaining new skills, but the introduction is a red herring in a bad direction. A reworked lead-in would draw the reader into a superbly intimate essay.

JACOB MERMELSTEIN

Sitting in an empty basement room for five hours at a stretch allows a lot of time for deep reflection. I had already gone through six months of weekly lectures by psychologists and other professionals and done countless role plays and practice calls in order to prepare for this moment, my first night manning the phones. Although it was past two in the morning, a mix of anxiety and excitement kept me jittery as I waited for my first call. In the back of my mind, I couldn't completely ignore the worry, "Why would anyone call an anonymous student-run peer-counseling hotline to talk to a complete stranger about their most personal issues?" A deeper fear (that I tried unsuccessfully to ignore) was whether I would be able to help them if they actually did call. In the next hour, both of my questions were answered. It was a call from a nervous freshman trying to recover from his parents' recent divorce and worried about classes, making friends, and fitting in at college. I was able to draw on the skills that I had learned during the intensive training and allay his fears, and by the end of that call I experienced the tremendous satisfaction of knowing that my training and preparation had allowed me to give immediate and direct help to someone in distress.

Both my experience at the counseling hotline, Nightline, and my coursework in my major in economics (including game theory) have fueled my fascination with the area of law concerned with alternative dispute resolution (ADR). At Nightline I learned to hone skills of active listening, feedback, analysis, and perception that I believe would be invaluable in the process of ADR. I was able to continue to employ the skills I learned at Nightline as well as learn more about ADR at my current job at the plaintiff-side employment law firm of Outten and Golden. As I frequently serve as the initial contact individuals have with the firm, I often find myself depending on my skills as a peer counselor in order to talk to individuals who are sometimes in very emotionally charged states after having just been fired from their long-term jobs. In addition, sitting in on weekly meetings as the attorneys discuss how to proceed in a matter, I have been able to gain a greater appreciation for the process of ADR. I have learned that individuals seldom make their objectives clear at the outset and often do not themselves have a firm grasp of their own position. A successful mediator, like a successful peer counselor, can identify what lies in the best interest of each side and encourage movement toward that goal. Moreover, every conflict or dispute is not a zero-sum game. That is, a gain for one side in a conflict does not always indicate a loss for the opposing side, as there are often conflict resolutions in which both sides can benefit. As game theory confirms, two opposing parties may make independent selfish decisions and as a consequence end up themselves worse off, while an independent outside party can sometimes find an outcome in which both parties can have a greater gain.

At the same time, my work at Outten and Golden has also taught me that there are disputes for which mediation would not be appropriate or in which it would be necessary to have binding arbitration, or actual litigation. For this reason I am eager to attend law school in order to learn the skills and acquire the knowledge that would allow me, when necessary, to act not only as a mediator, but also as an advocate and litigator. What appeals to me about Harvard Law School in particular is the possibility of receiving a strong general law education and also focusing on my particular area of interest, ADR. It is my fondest wish to be able to study with Professors [Robert] Mnookin and [Frank] Sander in their courses on negotiation and mediation. I am also drawn to the Harvard Mediation Program, which would allow me to have hands-on training and experience as a mediator. I believe Harvard is the ideal environment for developing both as a lawyer and a mediator, and if I were fortunate enough to be accepted I am confident I would be a dedicated, passionate, and constructive addition to the Harvard Mediation Program and the law school in general.

Review by Kyle L. K. McAuley

Mermelstein opens this essay dynamically with his fascinating account of working at a peer-counseling hotline. These interesting opening lines—a staple of virtually all good essays—get the reader interested and excited about the essay.

Mermelstein's essay is remarkable for its detailed emphasis on one particular area of law that its author is interested in. Mermelstein conveys at once his passion for negotiation, his experience with it in both the legal and service worlds, and why he thinks HLS will particularly help further his talents. This final paragraph, where he speaks of Harvard's negotiation experts and courses, is particularly convincing because it expresses a unique interest in Harvard without being a stock paragraph that he sends to all the schools he's applied to, just substituting "Harvard" for "Virginia" and "Stanford" along the way.

In the essay's body, however, Mermelstein abandons the descriptive and engrossing language of his introduction. He is clearly a very talented writer, but he lets those talents take the backseat to formulaic legalese. With so many other law school essays consisting of similarly indirect prose, Mermelstein's could have been a real standout if he had maintained his direct, descriptive style.

JOEL B. POLLAK

"It's time you learned to do things the Chicago way." That's what my father, a transplant surgeon, was told by his bosses when he complained about fraud in his hospital's liver transplant program. Several doctors, he discovered, had been exaggerating the severity of their patients' illnesses so that they would receive livers first, ahead of patients at other hospitals in the city. Not only was this practice illegal, but it put the lives of truly desperate patients at risk. Instead of taking immediate action to stop the wrongdoing, however, the administration demoted my father and cut his salary.

My father's only recourse was to turn to the legal system. In 1999, he and his lawyers approached a federal prosecutor. Four years later, the government announced that the hospital and two others in

Chicago had been caught cheating the organ allocation system. A settlement was reached, and my father was awarded a small amount in damages. The money barely covered his legal bills. But he had been vindicated.

Watching my father go through this ordeal and emerge victorious, I began to consider law as a serious career option. I had never been "prelaw"; I had always pursued my academic interests and work opportunities for their own sake. But I was inspired by the way my father's lawyers had helped him defend his principles and his career.

My father's case also resonated with my experiences as a political speechwriter and journalist in my native South Africa. I have witnessed many local examples of "the Chicago way," cases of corruption in government that have corroded the idealism of South Africa's young democracy. I began to see my father's struggles as similar to those of ordinary South Africans who dare to protest. My place, I felt, was among the men and women who defend such people and their ideals against injustice.

I had already begun to act as an advocate for a variety of different causes. In 2000, for example, I helped a woman in a squatter camp in Cape Town design and launch a website for her fledgling bed-and-breakfast—which happily is still in business today. In 2001, I published an op-ed in defense of the rights of the Inupiat Eskimos in Alaska, whom I had written about in my senior thesis and who were being overlooked in national debates about oil drilling in Alaska. Later that year, I tackled South Africa's minister of water affairs and forestry in a public debate about the Israeli-Palestinian conflict. I challenged his harsh anti-Israel views in letters and articles in national newspapers, and on one occasion we even debated each other in public.

My success emboldened me to take up other issues. In 2003, I presented a complaint of hate speech against South Africa's public broadcaster after a news announcer read out an e-mail alleging that Jews had conspired to launch the Iraq war. The panel of judges at the Broadcasting Complaints Commission found against me but commented, "The Complainant . . . very ably presented his case. He handed in a 42-page document, almost like Heads of Argument by counsel."

That same year, I was asked by my Arabic teacher to represent an Islamic school at a city planning hearing. The school wanted to build a facility in a new neighborhood, but some of the area's residents were opposed to the idea. I argued that South Africa's new constitution, which guarantees religious and cultural rights, would not permit the school to be blocked. Eventually, the school succeeded with its plans.

These endeavors have shaped my goals, and they have led me to law, with a political career as a long-term goal. They have also helped me define my values. Proud of my Chicago upbringing, I must yet lend my hand to the fight against "the Chicago way."

Review by Andrew C. Esensten

Pollak very effectively communicates in this essay why he wants to attend law school. He writes honestly about the role that lawyers played in helping his father combat corruption in Chicago and in sparking his interest in law as a possible career. Though Pollak devotes the first third of the essay to his father's ordeal— too much space for a short personal statement—he wisely uses the rest of the essay to address his own impressive accomplishments as a journalist and advocate.

Without even a hint of pretense or self-righteousness, Pollak describes a number of episodes in which he challenged authority in his native South Africa. He employs clear language and modesty in recounting these truly fascinating conflicts. However, by devoting no more than a few sentences to each one, Pollak misses an opportunity to discuss how his thoughts about law and justice evolved over time. The essay would be stronger if the author chose two or three conflicts and fully explored what he learned from them.

Despite this, Pollak's essay provides solid proof that he can write, argue, and speak in public—three skills that all lawyers (and politicians) must master if they hope to be successful. Pollak's admission that he did not follow the prescribed prelaw path but instead "pursued [his] academic interests and work opportunities for their own sake" is refreshing. Law schools are always looking for well-rounded candidates with real-life experience, and this essay demonstrates that Pollak fits the bill.

MATT SANCHEZ

I've never been one to follow conventional paths. Despite the urgings of my parents, advisers, and everyone else who knows what is best for me, I always have done things my own way.

At the University of Florida, advisers tell journalism students to seek internships at local newspapers. They say putting in your dues at a small publication will make you attractive to larger newspapers, which are the stable employers of the journalism world. So, most journalism students lined up at career fairs last year, hoping to snag one of said internships. I instead sent an e-mail directly to the editor of my favorite national magazine, *Bass Player*. After a two-month online correspondence, I convinced the editor to offer me a summer internship.

Those same journalism students also are told those local internships would involve a large amount of drudgery, with more glamorous responsibilities or even publication possible only after they put in the hard labor. It took me one day at *Bass Player* to convince the editors to allow me to interview one of my idols, who also is one of the most popular figures among members of the magazine's audience. The piece I put together from the interview went over well with the editors, and the magazine has published my articles in almost every issue since.

"I Want to Be a Lawyer Because..."

The summer before, I learned of an internship with a local left-wing, political-activist magazine. My views run moderate to conservative, save for some social issues, so the magazine and I seemed to be a perfectly inappropriate fit. I saw promise in the internship, however, and submitted my application. At the interview, I made no attempt to disguise my opinions, and I'm confident I expressed views that never before had been expressed in those offices. I began the internship a month later and served as co-managing editor for an issue of the magazine only a few months after that.

Given my successes in following my own path, the few moments in which I am denied [those successes] are all the more frustrating. Throughout my experiences with the various publications that have occupied the majority of my time outside of class, there has been a single recurring source of this frustration: the ability of public officials to hide information that is guaranteed to the public by law. Public records laws say one thing, administrators say another, and the requester loses nearly every time.

I believe that a law school education provides my only hope of relief from this metaphorical thorn in my side. While I cannot guarantee my path will not waver—in fact, you could say wavering, in one sense, is the only thing my path is guaranteed to do—I am committed to putting all of my efforts toward bringing about positive change in this aspect of the law. Newspapers, media outlets, and civic-minded citizens are refused access to public records every day by officials who have little fear of legal reprisal.

I realize one person cannot correct this. I realize few of these requesters have the resources to stage such legal battles. I also realize this certainly is not the most lucrative use of a law degree. This is, however, where my path has led me today, and no force thus far has managed to get between me and my chosen goals.

55 Successful Harvard Law School Application Essays

Review by Nikhil G. Mathews

Matt's essay does a very good job of demonstrating his desire to attend law school by rooting it in his past life experiences. In the process, he reveals much about himself, including his passion for journalism and the nonconformist tendencies he prides himself on. But his essay could have been made stronger by the addition of more colorful anecdotes and less of a linear summation of his résumé.

Matt opens his essay by introducing a distinctive trait about himself—daring—that will recur throughout the essay. This is an effective essay-writing tool because it strings together the different parts of his essay into one coherent piece.

Matt traces his journalistic successes, which he indicates flow from an ability to navigate unorthodox situations. He provides examples of journalistic victories he won despite seemingly adverse conditions, confirming the consistency and value of his bold approach to life. He should have elaborated on one of these stories, however. He tells us about the "recurring" source of frustration about public records, but leaves the point at that. Discussing one particular example of this, rather than mentioning that he has experienced many of them, would have been more effective.

The issue of public records law, however, is a great transition that allows Matt to draw the connection between his career as a journalist and his desire to pursue a law degree. As a journalist frustrated by opaque public records, he has realized the need for improvement of this field of law.

In pursuing this disciplined route to demonstrating his reasons for applying to law school, Sanchez accomplishes several tasks. First, he demonstrates that his interest in the law is substantive rather than whimsical. He deftly calls attention to his major extracurricular achievements without seeming immodest. Perhaps

"I Want to Be a Lawyer Because..."

most importantly he founds the entire essay on his essential trait of nonconformism, which he takes as his defining characteristic. He returns to this fundamental point in his conclusion, looking to the future with confidence that the daring that has produced success thus far will continue to reward him.

TRAVELS

Dharma Betancourt

The sun glints through my window on a shining San Juan morning, and I bask in the burning embrace of my own sweet light, beaming over Puerto Rico. The sun does indeed strike differently here. I remember the golden Boston sun of my college years, which was almost ornamental, emanating hardly any heat and bathing the world below in a shimmering aura, an unreal, fantastical glow. It was not the vibrant light that filled my childhood memories, stark and striking, always invigorating. And the pale blue sky was always a whispering echo of the turquoise canopy that filled my dreams.

And yet today I seek to leave again. Even as I enjoy the savory typical Christmas dishes and the balmy weather of the winter months, I know that these things are not enough to make me content. I left Puerto Rico in search of the extraordinary opportunities offered to me as a literature student at Harvard University. And now that I am back, I have started itching from wanderlust again—the prospect of the unknown, of the extraordinary, has always been alluring. "No man is an island, entire of itself," wrote John Donne. "[E]very man is a piece of the continent, a part of the main." This was a lesson I learned early on.

My taste for traveling and exploring was whetted and nourished primarily through reading as I was growing up. Some of my first memories involve reading fairy tales, myths, and Bible stories with my mother and three younger siblings, sitting at my father's side as he translated stories into Spanish, or being roused as he came home with a bag full of ten-cent books from the Salvation Army store. In subsequent years, I visited many lands and characters through my books; in discovering my passion for words, I lived a thousand lives across time and space.

By the time I graduated from high school, my traveling experience transcended my books—I had already been across the United States and to several Latin American countries with my family. I quickly became involved as press director with Harvard Model Congress Europe (HMCE), a conference for high-school students which models different government organizations of international relevance. I found it extremely rewarding to instill a sense of political and social awareness in the students through their coverage of the intricacies of U.S.-international relations as simulated by the program. This experience with HMCE also enabled me to travel to Paris and London. Furthermore, in the spring semester of my junior year I moved to Spain to study art history and literature, learning from my coursework, but also from visiting museums; going to the opera, restaurants, and shows; and wandering around the country and joining in the fray of impromptu celebrating. And at the end of the semester, I bought myself a cheap ticket to Rome, taking as my entire capital some four hundred dollars for three weeks.

My time away from the island has fundamentally changed the way I perceive my cultural identity vis-à-vis the United States and the Hispanic world. Puerto Ricans claim Hispanic heritage and Spanish as an integral part of our national identity. And yet our links to the rest of the Hispanic community are weak, whereas our infrastructures and our collective fate are intrinsically bound to the United States. I learned more about Latin America away from Puerto Rico by interacting closely with Hispanics from different national backgrounds than I had in all my previous years as a student. This strengthened my sense of vocation for law since I realized that as Puerto Ricans we are disenfranchised, that normal democratic channels are not available to us because of our peculiar relationship with the United States. There is still much room for a redefinition of the laws that gird Puerto Rico to the rest of the Union.

Travels

Today, I am committed to a career in law, but my passion for reading and writing, for the challenging and the intellectually stimulating, for advocacy and politics, had initially marked me for work as a journalist. As a high-school journalist, I was fascinated to learn that language, far from being a mere vehicle of communication, can also serve as a tool for chronicling and shaping history, public opinion, and the policy-making process. In my pursuit of journalism, I was driven by a desire to effect real change in the community through those snappy, juicy little articles I wrote and edited. I thus sought to work for organizations dedicated to raising public awareness of and proposing solutions to the problems and issues which plague our society. Yet an internship at *Newsweek*, a national magazine, and especially the election coverage I performed for the Associated Press convinced me that I was more interested in the crafting of public policy and law.

As I face a change in career paths, away from journalism and toward a legal practice, my continued aim is to craft documents with immediate impact, using my talent as a writer to improve the quality of public life. My work with the press has given me a sense of how public consciousness and opinion can shape the law, and has allowed me to cultivate qualities such as originality, keenness, the ability to work under pressure, and a commitment to the truth. It has also trained my writing specifically for precision and style, and so that it can serve as a sharper and finer tool for public service. Furthermore, my curriculum in college—ranging in courses from literature, foreign cultures and languages, government and history to moral reasoning, economics, religion, and anthropology—has given me analytical prowess and solid research skills. I want to use these skills more directly by being involved in politics and policy making through a legal career.

In the words of a Puerto Rican folk song, my heart stayed by the sea in Old San Juan, by the placid Caribbean shores. For now there is time, I feel, time for a hundred visions and revisions, to explore and learn, before I need to settle down. Eventually, however, I would like to return to Puerto Rico, using my talent and my education to forge significant social change and to improve the cultural and economic landscape on the island by bettering the international networks between the island and the rest of the world.

Review by Katherine M. Gray

Dharma discusses five different experiences that make her a good applicant: her reading, her international experience, her interest in United States–Puerto Rico interactions, her experience with the model congress, and her journalism career. Any one of these would make a fine essay, but she offers too little information about each of them by trying to incorporate them all. She probably felt she had to explain why her interest in law school and her experience did not match up, why she chose journalism internships and the model congress rather than legal internships or a mock trial.

Dharma's essay could have been much stronger had she focused on her thoughts and passions about Puerto Rico's relationship with the U.S. government, perhaps including a personal anecdote. She could then have discussed her involvement in the model congress, thus leading up to her interest in international law. While mentioning her passion for journalism may show her writing skills, it is something apparent in her CV and thus could be set aside to make room to expound on her other qualities.

Dharma should also be careful with the two quotes she incorporates in her essay; they're dynamic, but she doesn't fully explain their relevance—a single quote better tied to her theme would have worked far better.

CHLOE COCKBURN

Throughout my secondary-school and college careers, I cultivated parallel analytical and creative interests. At Harvard, this led to my decision to double major in classics and studio art. In some cases, the pursuit of two such disparate disciplines might limit one's ability to explore either in depth. On the contrary, I found that maintaining a serious interest in each of these two areas made me a more successful student in both. My two successful honors theses, with interconnected themes, were evidence of this.

After graduating in 2001, I decided to focus on either an analytical or a creative course of action. As the path of graduate studies in Greek did not satisfy my need to interact with the world outside of an institution, I resolved to explore the implications of my painting thesis. Thus, I moved to San Francisco, where I joined several Harvard friends in a large live/work warehouse and set up a studio there.

My time in San Francisco was fruitful. I developed a strong body of work, which I showed in five exhibitions. I also produced a large art project for the Burning Man arts festival, which takes place in the Nevada desert each August. In order to supplement my income from painting sales, I worked for SparkNotes as a writer/editor and for CyberEdit as an editor. These jobs allowed me to maintain and develop my analytical writing skills. I also tutored three high-school students in writing for one year.

After a year and a half in San Francisco, I yearned to return to the intensity of the East Coast. In early 2003, I moved to Brooklyn, where I painted at a far more advanced level than I had done before. However, while my immersion in the New York art world was a boon to the quality of my work, it also gave me pause as to the direction of my chosen career. Though I read feverishly as always, I found that I still lacked for adequate intellectual stimulation. Furthermore, outside events compelled me to look beyond my studio walls. I closely followed both the developments in Iraq and the domestic implications of the Patriot Act. The dissonance between my interests and my actions pushed me to a turning point: I decided to reconsider going to law school.

While my passion for painting has not lessoned, I know that I cannot happily work away in my studio while such radical changes are taking place in this country. I have the intellectual acuity and analytical training to engage the field of constitutional law; I know that nothing else will satisfy my desire to actualize my potential in the world. After spending two years pursuing the nonacademic path, I am keen to tear back into a rigorous course of study with far-reaching implications.

Review by Katherine M. Gray

Cockburn has written a tight and compelling personal statement which could be improved with anecdotes or concrete examples that she has a multifaceted intellect. The reader can glean most of the intriguing details described in the essay from her résumé. The essay is straightforward and reads smoothly, but it fails to give the reader a sense of her personality and personal experience.

Cockburn has an interesting point to make, but she takes too many paragraphs to reach it. Her essay is strongest when she writes that she is not exercising her talents to the fullest as an artist and wants to engage in political and constitutional discourse. Refocusing the essay along these lines and giving the reader a couple [of] moments or examples to support her claims would make for a stronger essay.

Although there is limited space in her personal statement, even giving more details about her artwork, the festival in Nevada, and her previous job experience would make for more lively and interesting writing.

DANA KING

Power has always fascinated me. As far back as I can remember, I have struggled to understand what it is, how it is assumed, and the ways in which it is wielded. My first years at Barnard College were spent in trying to change the power imbalances I saw around me. I immersed myself in a variety of activities both on and off campus. I helped to found the first women-of-color house on campus; helped to organize black Barnard women's participation in the Million Woman March, the Jericho Movement for political prisoners, and the campus campaign to end the embargo against Cuba, as well as working as a mentor and tutor with children in the Harlem community. My involvement in campus and community politics forced me to see the political nature of the difference between the luxury of my Ivy League institution and the dissipation of the surrounding Harlem community. My courses tended to interpret these differences in solely racial terms, relying heavily on the experiences of African Americans in the United States as the basis of a generalized worldview.

A year abroad at the University of Ghana during my junior year dramatically altered my understanding of power relations. It had been easy to accept oppression as a racialized experience while in the United States. However, faced with the overwhelming poverty of the majority of Ghanaians, a tiny black elite, and a political system engineered to keep that small minority in power, I could no longer buy simplistic arguments that pitted race against race. I began to understand that societal divisions were fundamentally based on access to resources, and that race was only one potential factor in determining access. While I have experienced discrimination as a black woman, for the first time I could not deny that my American passport alone afforded me access to spheres beyond the reach of most Ghanaians, such as free primary and secondary education. As I studied the economic history and development of Ghana, I learned more about the roles international forces had played in shaping national economic and political policies. Up until that point, my understanding of the power of international bodies to effect national policy formation had been relatively limited. As an American citizen, I had never experienced the harsh realities of structural adjustment plans handed down by extranational bodies such as the IMF and the World Bank. A brutal example of this during my stay was the University of Ghana ending its free tuition program for Ghanaian students. Watching the student protests against the Ghanaian government, I was unable to choose sides, as it became clear that the restructuring of the university system was not in the hands of the national leaders. Rather, it was a directive of international agencies that, as a condition to guaranteeing the aid and trade so critical to Ghana's economic survival, demanded the implementation of their development agendas.

Learning about the politics of international relations helped me to understand the frustration I had often felt as a student organizer at Barnard, where I rarely saw the tangible change that I was struggling for. While grassroots movements are effective on a local level, without the force of an international body behind them, they cannot move the international political and economic mechanisms by which wealth and rights are allocated. It is now clear to me that, as the world becomes increasingly globalized, those who are able to lobby for and effectuate policy change from an international level will be the most critical in determining the direction of national change and in establishing it. To this end, I am interested in studying law. I would like to study, and to one day have a hand in shaping, the policies that govern the interaction of international bodies with national governments. Going away helped me to understand that my commitment to equalizing the power imbalance—of international bodies and national governments; of human rights prerogatives and economic agendas—must be coupled with the ability to move within and understand the workings of the global structures that determine it.

Travels

Review by Lois E. Beckett

Dana's essay is a terrific example of how to showcase your diversity while presenting yourself as far more than just another minority candidate. Being an African American woman is clearly an important part of Dana's identity and is worth writing about. But rather than making that identity the sole focus of her essay, she places it within the broader context of power relations and shows how her self-understanding evolved during a trip abroad.

This essay draws its strength from its careful organization. The essay opens with the powerful first line, "Power has always fascinated me," and never loses sight of that theme. We are first introduced to power at the intersection of race and politics in America. But her introduction to Ghanaian society shows Dana a power inequality that has nothing to do with race, and forces her to reconsider whether black Americans are disadvantaged on a worldwide scale. From there, Dana transitions smoothly to a broader consideration of power on a national and international level in Ghana, as demonstrated by the IMF's pressure on the Ghanaian education system.

Rather than lambast the IMF, Dana takes a nuanced stance and places her desire to study law within the context of international power relations: she wants to understand, and ultimately change, these organizations. Anyone can say they want to eliminate power imbalances, but Dana's treatment of the topic is proof she has considered the issue and will be an effective advocate for constructive change.

Writing about how your most fundamental ideas have changed is a great essay topic. It shows admissions officers that you are perceptive and able to think critically about your own experiences, while also giving them a sense of your worldview. If, as Dana did, you can tie all this together with why you want to be a lawyer, you have a recipe for a successful essay.

REGINA FITZPATRICK

Rwanda wasn't supposed to be real. I had studied the 1994 genocide in Rwanda fervently in the hope of discovering whether societal recovery was possible. The scenario in Rwanda seemed to be the ultimate test of human resilience. But thinking about a phenomenon is not the same as picturing it. Maybe it is too far away conceptually to be tangible. Ultimately, all of my background knowledge could not have adequately prepared me for the complexity of the situation on the ground.

My first impression of Rwanda is that it looks like any other place I have ever been. The drive into Kigali overwhelms me; it is a bustling capital city in every sense. Having lived in a small town in Tanzania for a while, I am startled. I see a streetlight and realize I have not seen one in three months. There are French restaurants, a movie theater, and excellent roads. And there are so many people. The high population density of Rwanda is something that I have read about, yet have trouble grasping. I expected to see a decimated society. But even outside Kigali, navigating the winding roads of rural Rwanda, there are people everywhere—farming, riding bikes, loitering. The number of children under the age of eight is particularly remarkable to me. I wonder if they are products of rape, or orphans. Or is there just a natural desire to replenish society after such devastation? Staring at these children, there is something missing. Usually when you smile at children, they smile back. These do not, not easily. I am curious [about] how much they know about their past.

As days pass, my preconceptions continue to be invalidated. Initially, I was intellectually attracted to the Rwandan genocide precisely because it seemed straightforward, with identifiable "good guys" and "bad guys." The Tutsis, being the victims and the victors, were obviously the "good guys." The current Tutsi-dominated regime faces unprecedented challenges in rebuilding a shattered society, and is granted moral authority and wide latitude in doing so. The Hutus, having followed their leaders to bloody, unfathomable extremes, were obviously the "bad guys." While hundreds of thousands of perpetrators are incarcerated, the remainder of the population is encouraged to reconcile. However, now I find there is more to the story; for the first time, I am exposed to the non–politically correct edition.

When Rwandans talk about the past, they generally refer to "the war" rather than "the genocide," because the events of 1994 are not isolated in their minds. A myriad of unspoken, complicated nuances of discourse has emerged to avoid assumptions. For example, speaking to someone in English shows you think they are Tutsi, raised in Uganda, and affiliated with the current government. Likewise, the innocent question "Where are you from?" cannot be answered without alluding to the individual's role in the genocide. If the answer is anywhere in Rwanda, it raises the question of how he or she survived. The most common nuance of discourse is silence, but the sheer silence of the majority speaks volumes.

The critical thinker in me begins to realize the truth lies somewhere in the middle of the extreme versions. The heralded current regime appears not to be as angelic as depicted. Evidence has surfaced that its armed forces committed war crimes and crimes against humanity during the civil war and ensuing refugee crisis. To this day, basic human rights are routinely abused and independent thought stifled. Political opponents, labeled "divisionists," are deprived of due process; international observers question the fairness of elections; and eight years after extremist radio incited a population to genocide, there is still only one radio station in the country. Clearly the current government is the "good guy" relative to the extremists who presided over genocide. However, the fact that the regime can still be so "bad" naturally lends credence to its opponents. Both sides have their share of saints and demons, and the vast majority of the population cannot afford the luxury of "sides," as it struggles for survival. Now I can appreciate why there has been no history curriculum taught in the nation's schools for the last decade.

Joseph, my interpreter here, is one of many Rwandan victims. He is a friend of a friend and a recent law graduate from the National University. Joseph is also a genocide survivor, one of the few Tutsis I met who was actually in Rwanda in 1994. His reserve and cautious nature, though understandable, make me uncomfortable. Nonetheless, I am impressed by Joseph. He speaks freely and criticizes the status quo, both rare practices in Rwanda. He does so not with passion or zeal, but with a sincere thoughtfulness that is compelling. He refuses to join the survivors' organizations in Rwanda because, after suffering discrimination for so many years, he vows never to inflict it on anyone else. Although I find myself wondering why there cannot be more Josephs in Rwanda, maybe it is for the best. For all his ideals and compassion, Joseph has no hope. He fears an impending return to conflict, seeks to escape his people's cyclical fate, and refuses to expose any future children to such a society.

Now that Rwanda is real to me, I consider Joseph's pessimism. I aspire to find the best way forward, and yet, like him, I wonder if there is any hope. I do not expect law school to make everything simple again, but I do seek to gain tools and perspective with which to respond to such pessimism. Joseph is a "good guy," and he wants out. That does not bode well for Rwanda.

Review by Kenneth Saathoff

This is an extremely gripping essay from the very first sentence, which plunges us into the author's puzzlement and distress over the Rwanda situation. The essay continues with clear, well-crafted sentences that are both insightful and evocative. Regina's story is engrossing, and her use of the present tense allows us to experience with her; to almost watch Kigali unfold before us. By showing us how her preconceived notions were continually proved untrue, she showed us the value of actually traveling to Rwanda, rather than simply studying it from an academic standpoint. She shows a keen eye for observing her surroundings, as illustrated by her comment on the unsmiling children.

Regina understands the horrors of the genocide, but also presents herself as a sophisticated thinker and analyst. Without overlooking the Hutus' crimes, she recognizes shades of gray and searches for meaning within that context. In what makes up the strongest part of the essay, she examines the way contemporary society has been affected by the genocide, and how even asking simple questions brings up an awkwardness that would be unexpected by outsiders. Her sentence "The most common nuance of discourse is silence, but the sheer silence of the majority speaks volumes" is extremely powerful, making a unique connection and clearly painting a picture of the environment.

She wraps up the essay with a strong conclusion, as Joseph's perceptions of his country, in the context of [Regina's] entire visit to Rwanda, lead to her revealing the nature of her interest in the law. An "I want to go to law school because . . ." sentence is rendered unnecessary—the body of the essay has already answered that question.

KENNETH GARRETT

"Kenny, you're going to hell!"

It was just before I started college, and my recently "born-again" childhood friend, Leonard, was absolutely serious—he believed I was destined to eternal damnation because I did not share his newly embraced faith. My reaction reflected what I now know to have been a significant deficiency in my intellectual maturity: it was easier to dismiss Leonard as an irrational sub-intellectual than to allow any consideration of or respect for his beliefs. Though I regret it now, we didn't speak again for five years.

My reaction to Leonard's profession of absolute faith was not unique. In fact, this sort of intellectual immaturity is most often excused—even championed—as intellectual sophistication. "We" are enlightened, while "they" are provincial, so we need only to ignore them. It was possible to ignore those with passionate religious beliefs right up until a criminal few crashed two airliners into the World Trade Center as a misguided expression of faith.

At college I began to actually listen for the first time to the sandwich-boarded evangelist screaming and frothing near the post office. I stopped closing my blinds and ducking when the Jehovah's Witnesses came to the door. I resisted the urge to politely pretend I didn't notice the prayer rug my friend Ibrahim kept under his bed. I developed an insatiable thirst to ask all these people, "Why do you do it?" The mistake of ignoring Leonard, coupled with subsequent world events, taught me that a full understanding of the human condition requires an examination of religious fealty as much as it requires the study of economic or biological imperatives. My undergraduate years broadened the scope of my inquiries, but left me needing to know much more.

An in-depth study of religion in an international context seemed my best next step, so I spent a year at the University of Edinburgh Divinity School in Scotland with the idea that I might pursue a Ph.D. As I trekked daily through icy cobbled streets past statues of David Hume and John Knox, I considered the great variety of knowledge cultivated in that birthplace of the Enlightenment, and I realized that a focus on religion would be too narrow. What interests me is not religion per se, but its intersection with secular life. How does a society allow freedom and tolerance of religious expression while ensuring that religious practice does not interfere with the rights of others?

It is this question that has brought me to the doorstep of Harvard Law School. It is the law—separate from yet cognizant of religious passion—that strikes this balance. To fully understand the potential impact of human zeal, religious or otherwise, I need an understanding of systems of law and government, and how the law is intended and implemented to influence human behavior. Religion is but one of many variables explaining human conduct; it is the law that must take all of these variables into account, singularly and in relation to one another.

I could attend any number of law schools to simply prepare myself for the practice of law, but Harvard is one of very few institutions at which I could become a true legal scholar. Harvard's collegial atmosphere allows students and faculty to focus on a cooperative pursuit of knowledge, rather than on destructive competition. Harvard's programs in legal and constitutional history and external studies would prepare me for a possible career in academia, while Harvard's principles and practice program and broad array of classes and clinics would equip me to succeed wherever my interests lead, from corporate ethics, to a government advisory position, to the prosecution of perpetrators of religious genocide.

Leonard and I met again last month at a mini-reunion. I was delighted both to learn that he has moderated his voice and to share how I have grown since our last encounter. That our friendship has revived shows that the future is full of unexpected developments, and that those intellectually and spiritually prepared are in a position to take advantage of them. The preparation for a career and for life provided by Harvard Law would enable me to meet my future with intellectual maturity and a desire to pursue the truth to the benefit of both myself and society.

Review by Sarah McKetta

The first line of this piece is a great one—it engages the reader and immediately sets the tone for the rest of the essay. The author's voice really comes through: this essay is easygoing and conversational, not stiff and academic. It is written as if it is designed to be read aloud, an attribute you should strive for in your essay. This makes the story entertaining for the reader, and gets its point across well.

The topic is well chosen. By discussing a mistake he made in judging his friend, Kenneth demonstrates a capacity to accept and learn from his mistakes. By using this example, he highlights his personal attributes without ever naming them explicitly. This is a hallmark of a strong essay: *show* your strengths through examples, rather than simply telling us them. And while his accounts of meeting Jehovah's Witnesses and a Muslim friend demonstrate his strength of character, they do not come at the expense of including any academic information—he still goes into detail about his Ph.D. program. But again, the program is not mentioned as simply another notch in his belt; rather, it explains his jump from a student of divinity to one of law.

As you write your essay, be sure to make it come full circle, as Kenneth does. Just as the piece begins with his friend Leonard, so too does it end with him. We have followed Kenneth through several years of development, and he has demonstrated that he is a changed man.

SHANE HACHEY

The experience that has probably had the most significant impact on how I view the world and my place in it was my nine-month deployment to the former Yugoslavia from 1995 to 1996. My military police unit was attached to the NATO Implementation Force designed to enforce the provisions of the Dayton Peace Accords. My initial reaction was far from enthusiastic: not only did I question the value and wisdom of sending American soldiers to keep the peace in a part of the world that had decided to tear itself apart, but I had also grown up among Vietnam veterans, my father having broken his back in an accident that ended up saving him from being sent to Hamburger Hill. This military experience tends to make one cynical to say the least.

I was an M60 gunner, the one sticking out of the top of the Humvee. The gunner is a favorite of snipers and the first one to be picked off in a firefight, and I have to admit to a certain level of fear and selfishness when I considered the prospect that the peace was only temporary and that the Yugoslav combatants would decide to demoralize our forces by slowly picking away at our troops in the same fashion as the Vietnamese or the Somalis who wanted us out of their countries. It wasn't so much that I was afraid of dying, as real as that fear was. It was more that I was afraid of dying for nothing or for the wrong thing. As the deployment drew closer, the talk of whether our leaders knew what they were doing and if they had any idea of what we were going through dominated our conversation.

Upon arriving in Croatia and while performing my duties there and in Bosnia, I was struck by several things. The first was the level of poverty. My American imagination was completely inadequate to prepare me for the desperate living conditions of many of these people. Intrinsic poverty was widespread enough, and the war had only made things worse. To me, poverty meant trailer parks and government assistance programs, but for the people in Croatia and Bosnia poverty meant no running water (with every discomfort that entails) and growing your own food. Piled on top of this of course was the destruction: as I drove through one town I could see how somebody in the hills to my right had used his position to reduce the village on my left to rubble. I was frequently saddened by the lingering hostility I witnessed in survivors and became starkly aware of my sheltered experience. It's easy and common for Americans to judge others for ethnic hostility, but most modern Americans can scarcely imagine the ethnic tensions and fears associated with living within close proximity of people whom you know or suspect want you dead because of your race or religion.

All of which is to say that I was wrong. Wrong about the mission being a waste of time, wrong about it not being worth risking the lives of people foreign to the conflict, and mostly just wrong about it being none of my business. I realized that most of the victims of the conflict were innocent bystanders and that the popular "Let them kill each other" logic associated with noninvolvement failed to take this into account. I also realized that America and our allies were in a unique position to positively influence world affairs, and that to passively observe a slaughter, as we in the West tend to do, is to waste an opportunity to use our position to help people other than ourselves. It occurred to me that it is utterly hypocritical of us to speak of American leadership and at the same time be afraid of exercising the responsibility and taking the risks that come with leadership. In other words, NATO had arrived in Yugoslavia two years too late, and I found myself not only eager for my mission, but regretful that I had not arrived earlier.

This experience, besides clarifying and widening my understanding of the world I live in, fanned the flames of a nascent interest in international policy and foreign affairs. Having witnessed the consequences of failed diplomacy and international cooperation, I have committed myself to a career in international law so that I might someday play a part in helping the international community prevent such tragedies and [so that I might] have a hand in bringing war criminals to justice. The experience and knowledge I would gain from a legal education at Harvard would be an invaluable contribution to my goal, and I would embrace the opportunities and challenges presented to me should I be accepted. Whichever road I take, I intend to do everything I can to ensure that in the future no American soldier will have to see the look on someone's face that says, "You're too late."

Review by Brittney L. Moraski

Though this applicant's opening could have been rewritten to sound less generic and tentative, his essay is interesting and engaging because of the uniqueness of his experience. While many applicants may write of their desire to work to bring justice to war-torn parts of the world, this applicant has actual experience of doing so, which he wisely highlights in his essay. In his way, he is able to separate himself from other applicants, and his essay gives the admissions committee an idea of what his contributions would be like in the classroom. Not many students, for instance, are likely to have the experience of being the "favorite of snipers and the first one to be picked off in a firefight."

The weaknesses in this essay come not from its content but from its structure. The opening could be reworked to grab the reader's attention more quickly (additionally, the "probably" in the first sentence is unnecessary, muddling up the development of the essay), and the ending comes on a little too quickly to make the strong impact the applicant had intended. Applicants with unique experiences to write about should employ anecdotes rather than descriptions in their essay to make a stronger impression, which this applicant could also use more to his advantage. Because the essay is a rare opportunity to inject a personal element into the admissions process, it is important to include details and experiences that will make it easier for the admissions committee to see an applicant not as a collection of adjectives, but as a real person.

KATHARINE MAPES

It would be easy to say that living and traveling in the Middle East taught me what poverty is or what war is. And, from a certain point of view, it would be true. It was in Egypt that I saw real, crushing poverty for the first time. It was in Beirut that I saw entire blocks desiccated by shelling, and it was in Jerusalem that I saw a city inundated by a military presence, coping with a daily string of casualties on all sides. However, if that was all I came away with, I would be doing the people and the region a horrible disservice. There were also wedding parties that filled the streets with people and music and laughter, beautifully rebuilt districts next to monuments of staggering antiquity, and hundreds of people moved to tears by the presence of the Western Wall or the Dome of the Rock or the Church of the Holy Sepulchre.

I spent most of my year abroad studying in Cairo, and it was Cairo that left the greatest impression of all. A lot of people have written a lot of things about Cairo. Usually, they emphasize the bustle, the activity, the sheer energy the place exudes. My own accounts are hardly different. Here's what I wrote late one night in my apartment on the outskirts of Giza: "It should be jarring to have a Chili's and an Applebee's in a city where ten thousand mosques sound the call to prayer five times a day and where ancient monuments tower just out of sight. But it's not. Instead, it just contributes to a sense of place stronger and more moving than any I've felt in cities more beautiful, but less distinct." It was this contrast of old and the new, Western and Eastern, that really captured me. I went to Egypt with little idea of what to expect; in the wake of September 11, the Middle East was relevant and exciting. By the time I left a year later, I was in love. I read voraciously about the region's politics and culture and history. I devoted myself to Arabic, signing up for a class on Islamic texts. In short, I learned that not only did I want to work with the Middle East, but also that I had become intertwined with it.

At around the same time, I began to develop an interest in international rights law, particularly as it relates to humanitarian crises and refugee flows. As an intern at the State Department's Bureau of Population, Refugees, and Migration, I researched the problems pertaining to refugee women, wrote recommendations concerning Temporary Protected Status designations, evaluated programs aimed to assist displaced children, and participated in conference calls with public health personnel in the field in Iraq. This experience built my awareness both of the character and magnitude of these crises and of the policy remedies that are often applied. At the American University in

Travels

Cairo the next spring, I took a graduate-level seminar on international refugee law that taught me about the legal aspects of humanitarian crises, and also the ways in which the law can be used not only to sanction but [also] to assist. After I returned, I volunteered at a nonprofit organization that assists low-income clients with immigration proceedings, and this gave me a view of, it could be said, the other end of the process: what happens to migrants who have reached their destinations. These intellectual and professional experiences have solidified my commitment to studying international human rights law. Harvard's vast array of courses and programs that focus on international human rights and public-interest law topics make it an ideal place to pursue my interests and continue on the path that I started on when I took my first Arabic class, when I started at the State Department, and when I got off the plane at Cairo International Airport.

Review by Sahil K. Mahtani

Katharine's essay follows in the the long tradition of American love affairs with the Middle East. She is quite aware of this, ensuring in the very first paragraph that readers won't stereotype her; she [indicates] she is not about to write a "how I discovered crushing poverty" essay. The thread of self-awareness continues in the second paragraph, when Katharine notes what typical descriptions of Cairo are, then professes her agreement with them. The extended quotation from her journal is beautifully employed because (1) it conveys her habit of writing down impressions regularly, an intelligent yet personally relevant activity, and (2) it provides a sense of romantic passion in doses unusual for admissions essays.

The description of her interest in international law is detailed (perhaps overly so, given that the information should be available on her résumé), but lacks imagery or examples illustrating just how close these experiences brought her to the reality of the lives of refugees. As it stands, her words do not convey the level of passion Katharine probably feels for the Middle East. That is to say, the second paragraph fails to live up to the promise of the first.

However, the language, for the most part, is very good. It manages to be detailed without being boring, clear but never redundant. Some of the images communicated are quite vivid ("wedding parties that filled the streets" and "ten thousand mosques sound the call to prayer"), and through those images, we can see the intensity of her experience in the Middle East. Structurally, the essay is really two essays in one, although the transition works. Despite the misuse of a word ("desiccated" means "dried up"; perhaps Katharine means "desecrated"), Katharine's essay is admirable for the balance it strikes between inner awareness and outer exploration.

CARRIE MEYERS

"*Tu peux entrer mais n'apporte pas la piqûre, s'il te plait,*" I pleaded with Clarise from behind the locked door of our bedroom. I was sick with a virus that had given me a fever, was making my nose bleed every time I stood up, and was wreaking havoc on my digestive system. In an effort to help me, the midwife with whom I shared a workplace, house, and double mattress on the floor was preparing to give me an injection of penicillin. While the possibility of relief that the antibiotic offered me was beyond appealing, I was afraid of HIV transmission through a questionably sanitary needle. I was telling Clarise that I would let her in if she would please not bring the syringe with her. She consented but wondered aloud why I would refuse her assistance and thereby remain too weak to work with her at the local clinic where she served as the only midwife or physician for a seventy-five-kilometer radius.

A villager that I met later on my daily trip into the rain forest to collect manioc root pleaded equally adamantly with me, this time to use traditional medicine. She held out a piece of charcoal and asked me to put it up my nostril as a preventative. Despite her persistence, I did not comply and instead held the charcoal piece at the edge of my nose. I had gone to Noé out of a desire to learn from and, if possible, assist an African woman who was very committed to working for social justice in her community. However, I found myself worrying about offending this friendly village woman and the midwife I worked for. I wondered how I could explain my rejection of their efforts to help me, especially since they were my elders and also my hosts. I was relieved when, a day after my recovery, I was welcomed back to the clinic and asked to help with a labor and delivery.

My experience living in Noé, a small village on the border of Côte d'Ivoire and Ghana with no running water or electricity, was certainly memorable. It was, however, only one of many international experiences that I have had. Consequently, I sometimes find that I feel as "at home" living overseas as I do in the United States. Wherever I am, I find meaning and a sense of purpose in discussing, observing, and most of all, in *doing* work in the area of social justice.

My interest in international justice issues was first sparked when I was seven, when my parents' involvement in international education took us to Guadeloupe, a small group of islands in the French West Indies. While living there, I attended first through third grade at a small French school. I remember feeling puzzled and upset about the difference in treatment given to children of different racial and ethnic backgrounds by our teachers. I continued to develop my interest in race, gender, class, and other issues later, as I attended three international schools in Germany, Côte d'Ivoire, and mainland China. College courses, visits to family or friends, and my position at Mennonite Central Committee also took me to numerous other countries in Europe, the Middle East, West Africa, Central and South America, and Southeast Asia.

One tangible result of my experiences is that I am proficient in

French, German, Spanish, and Mandarin. (I have lost most of the Creole and Agni that I once knew.) I also feel very at home in a variety of environments. In a sense, it seems as normal to me to be asked by women in Côte d'Ivoire to "marry them" (meaning marry their husband and become their co-wife), to be the only white child in a theatrical production on slavery given on cable TV in the Caribbean, or to watch masked villagers dance on stilts during traditional festivals in the Chinese countryside, as it does to live amidst the cornfields, quilting circles, and Hoosier basketball games of my "hometown" in northern Indiana.

One final, major influence on my life and interests is the Mennonite community in Goshen, Indiana—the community that I continually returned to in the United States. The environment of this ethnic subculture imbued me with a passion for social justice, a desire to live simply, and a sense of the deep value of personal relationships.

The law school–graduate school environment is foreign to me, with new cultural norms and an unfamiliar language—the language of the law. I want to do a joint degree in law and international relations because I see this degree as a vehicle that can be used to address inequities. In the Mennonite community, at the clinic in a West African village where I once volunteered, and in many other places around the world, people are seeking a more equitable world order. My background has given me the drive to learn the rules of the Western world—i.e., the law—in hopes of working within the Western system of order to help create a more just world.

Review by Brittney Moraski

In this essay, Meyers tackles what might be her most obvious weakness: her lack of legal experience. But rather than starting off by defending her inexperience, Meyers wisely chooses instead to begin her essay in Africa, far from the law offices where many of her peers slaved away. She waits until her final paragraph, after she has outlined her rich experiences, to point this out: "The law school–graduate school environment is foreign to me, with new cultural norms and an unfamiliar language—the language of the law."

Meyers's essay is effective because she does not present her international experiences as a laundry list of trips and countries—instead, she describes the marriage offers she received from Côte d'Ivoirian women, her performance as a child in Caribbean cable TV productions, festivals in rural China, and quilting circles in Indiana, thus illustrating the various experiences that make up her life in a much more evocative way than any résumé could. Her experiences are presented in a natural, not strained or self-serving, way and present Meyers as an interesting person who would have a lot to add in an academic setting.

Meyers's essay is a fine example of how a student with limited legal experience might approach his or her application essay. By using the bulk of her essay to explain to the admission committee how she has thus far lived her life ("Wherever I am, I find meaning and a sense of purpose in discussing, observing, and most of all, in *doing* work in the area of social justice"), Meyers makes an appropriate segue into explaining why she wants to attend law school: "My background has given me the drive to learn the rules of the Western world—i.e., the law—in hopes of working within the Western system of order to help create a more just world."

RYAN ROWBERRY

The years 2002 and 2003 have seen many firsts for China: entrance into the WTO, human space travel, a massive SARS outbreak that crippled tourism and business, and a terrorist explosion that rocked Peking University, China's premier tertiary educational institution.

On February 25, 2003, I was in the middle of explaining debate methods to my class of sophomore English majors at Peking University, when a bomb was detonated in the main student dining hall. My students and I rushed outside to see billowing smoke surrounding the dining hall and shattered glass littering the pavement. The scene was one of general chaos, with students flocking to see the destruction while young, rurally conscripted security guards formed a haphazard human police line to keep the crowds at bay. Reporters were soon on the scene, and it was evident from the frantic speaking and gesturing that, although no one was harmed, everyone was in a state of shock.

We discussed the explosion in class over the next few days, and it was my turn to be shocked when I discovered that the overwhelming majority of my students were gleeful about the bombing. In the words of one student from Chongqing, "It makes PKU more famous." As my students explained, Confucius taught that any events that bring fame, honor, and recognition should be viewed with happiness. Clearly, Confucian thought was still prevalent in China, despite the passing of two millennia since the death of the venerable sage. Furthermore, as I listened to students relate family stories detailing the gruesome Nanjing Massacre, rampant starvation during Mao's Great Leap Forward, and the public derision and rural "reeducation" of their parents' generation, I understood that a harmless explosion in a cafeteria was trivial in this context.

A few weeks after the bombing, Chinese headlines proclaimed that the perpetrator of the explosion had been captured. My students again caught me off guard. "He didn't do it," insisted a female student. "He probably committed another minor crime, and the government cut a deal with him." I pressed her further, and she explained, "If the government did not catch this criminal in a matter of weeks, they would 'lose face' in the eyes of the public. Therefore, the government apprehended this man and claimed he was the criminal." Almost every student in class agreed with her, and when I asked them about the administration of law and order in China, another student said, "The law in China is the will of those in power."

Although the discussions surrounding the explosion at Peking University taught me much about law, cultural practices, and attitudes in today's China, it was certainly not the only time I had encountered complex international issues. Over games of ping-pong (where the net consisted of a battered two-by-four) in a safe house for African political refugees in Nienburg, Germany, I learned about severe religious, legal, and political tensions that existed between Christian and Muslim tribes in Nigeria. Questioning Javier Solana on the floor of the Hungarian parliament about legal challenges to NATO's bombing raids in Bosnia reentrenched the fact that almost all countries are united culturally and politically to other countries. Studying international and comparative education in a multinational cohort at Oxford University helped me realize that curriculum, content, and administration of educational systems are heavily influenced by unique historical and cultural mores. And my current employment, in which I research domestic and international corporate accountability (specifically, Ford Motor Company's complicity during World War II with the use of slave labor in its German subsidiary, Ford-Werke), has also revealed that certain corporate entities wield greater economic and political clout than many nations. All of these experiences have deepened my understanding of international legal issues and the intricate relationships that frame them.

However, the most poignant lesson I have gleaned from my travels, education, and experiences abroad is that I am largely ignorant of several significant factors that have shaped and are currently shaping the United States of America and foreign nations. This ignorance has prompted me to apply to law school. I want to examine the United States and other nations through the lens of their respective legal systems and statutes, for law is one product of a nation's inherent values or, at least, the values of those in power. I am fascinated by the history of nations and relationships between nations, and I want to discover how these bonds or barriers have influenced international law and human rights. Thus, I plan to create a law degree combining three areas of study: international law, comparative law, and legal history. Ultimately, I view this law degree as a critical step toward teaching law. I am confident that the skills I develop from studying and practicing law, combined with the knowledge and teaching experience that I already possess, will enable me to assist future students in comprehending laws and legal systems within their historical contexts.

Review by Melissa Quino McCreery

Rowberry's extraordinary, compelling experiences are clearly his strength. His essay is effective, however, not because he can make an interesting catalogue of anecdotes but because his stories drive the essay and make his point for him.

Rowberry tailors his storytelling to fit his needs. The bombing of Peking University takes up the first half of his essay, and he focuses on what he learned by highlighting a single incident. This first story must double as a gripping introduction and as a "what I learned from my experience" piece. The rest of the accounts only need to fill the latter role, and so he focuses on the overarching lessons he took away and adds just a splash of colorful detail like the battered two-by-four.

The drawback to his structure is that the essay's purpose is not stated until the last paragraph. Rowberry does not need to mention law school sooner, but beginning the essay with a broad statement about China somewhat mischaracterizes its purpose. The essay succeeds because the stories are enthralling enough to keep their audience's attention until Rowberry makes his point, but it is not necessarily a sound strategy.

Once he reaches it, the conclusion is powerful because it illustrates that his hopes and expectations for law school fit into the aspirations he is already pursuing. Of course Rowberry wants to go to law school and thinks he can make unique contributions. Every applicant does. But Rowberry succeeds because by the time he says so, his storytelling has done its work: his assertion not only rings true, but it seems obvious.

CLIMBING THE MOUNTAIN

JAMES AHLERS

As a boy, I tended to fall asleep suddenly in unusual places. I once fell asleep as I crawled up the stairs of the family home, my upper body just onto the carpeted landing of the second floor. I once fell asleep at the bottom of a slide in our backyard in broad daylight. Then there was the time I disappeared for hours while my mom and dad, siblings, and neighbors searched for me frantically. I was blissfully unaware of the fuss as I slept under the couch.

I used to think that I must have had narcolepsy. Now I think that I was just bored.

I have with great effort continued to fight this affliction in adulthood as a college student attending accounting classes, a reporter covering aimless city council hearings, and a bureaucrat sitting through interminable meetings. I do my best to avoid such pointless activities because my parents taught me to live with a sense of purpose. Also, falling asleep in public is embarrassing.

The restless pursuit of new and purposeful challenges has taken me down many unexpected paths. Since I graduated from college, I've had at least three careers. I reported on some of the most important Latin American political events of our time and translated speeches for the president of Chile before I turned twenty-five. I became press secretary to the governor of Arizona before I turned thirty. Best of all, I've met extraordinary people of all kinds.

I began my professional life at age twenty-one as a newspaper reporter in Indiana, next door to my native Ohio, where I had spent my entire life. The job didn't last long. I couldn't ignore a growing desire to get out of the Midwest, so I quit and went to Chile. I still smile when I remember the warning that an editor gave me: "You're going to ruin your career."

I arrived in Santiago, Chile, in April 1995. I had a single friend and a single goal: to become fluent in Spanish. I started out teaching English, then became a magazine reporter and a correspondent for Voice of America, chronicling the country's growing pains as it sought to restore full democracy. I became a translator, translating speeches for the president of Chile, reports for the United Nations, and wine labels for export companies. I traveled the country, had my share of romance and good cheap wine, and made friendships like none I'd ever had.

I returned to Ohio in 1998 with the goal of moving to a city where I could continue to use my Spanish. I landed a reporting job at a newspaper in Phoenix, Arizona, covering international trade and the Latino business community. I was fortunate to win several journalism awards in 1999, among them two for stories about the death of a migrant construction worker who was sent into a trench without proper safety equipment. The stories helped change Arizona law. As one of my co-workers said at the time, "This kind of story is why we become journalists."

But I became increasingly jaded—and, yes, bored—by the lowest common denominator mentality that seemed to drive the media. After cranking out, assembly-line style, what seemed like my millionth story about the rise and fall of gasoline prices in Phoenix, I could take no more.

Luckily, my coverage of international trade opened the door for me to join the Arizona governor's office as a Mexico policy analyst in 2000. This post introduced me to the world of diplomacy and gave me the intellectual challenge I had been wanting. My responsibilities included serving as liaison to Spanish-language media, which led to my appointment as press secretary to the governor in the fall of 2002, as the governor was closing out her final term. I knew the November election would bring another change for me, but I made the most of the opportunity and did what I could to polish the governor's image at a difficult time.

I have since landed at the Arizona Office of Tourism as a "flak," which is what the media like to call us public relations people because we're the political equivalent of bullet stoppers. When I was a reporter, I swore I would never be a flak. I would be disappointed in myself if I hadn't come to understand since then that flaks, too, can serve a purpose. I was reminded starkly of that fact this January when I was assigned to be one of the state's public information officers handling media coverage of a hostage situation at an Arizona prison. If we failed to control the media frenzy, we were told, the hostages could end up dead. We did our part and the negotiators did theirs, and the hostages got out alive. It was the most difficult and rewarding task of my life.

I can't imagine what life will bring next, but I'm staying wide awake to find out.

Review by Nicholas K. Tabor

What's true for a newspaper article is true for an application essay: a good introduction is key, and James definitely has one. His description of his childhood pseudonarcolepsy is punchy, eloquent, and amusing; like all good writing, it conveys his passions for learning and doing new things without him having to state those interests directly. The narrative demonstrates an important personality trait, with a charming and innocent story that sweetens the essay. As you write your own essay, you should work similarly to grab your reader's attention. An anecdote grabs the attention of the reader, a vital result given how many application essays admissions officers must read and how little time they have to read them.

James spends the remainder of his personal statement fleshing out the details of his professional career—details that he would have already submitted on his résumé. Exploring postcollege activities is a wise way to approach the essay, but only when the exploration reveals something about why the activities were meaningful. In an essay there's a fine line between drawing on your life experiences and summarizing them, and James unfortunately does the latter. He provides less of an exploration than a laundry list, peppering the essay with self-serving quotations like the one about his newspaper editor in Ohio.

Lost in the body is the theme of narcolepsy, and the point of the introduction becomes lost on the reader. He returns back to it only at the very end, and then only tangentially and unconvincingly. Although it demonstrates his accomplishments well, the essay leaves us understanding James as a résumé grubber (albeit an extremely well credentialed one).

ERIC BENSON

My alarm went off at 5:30 on Saturday morning. I reluctantly climbed out of bed, pulled on my boots, and asked myself how Andy talked me into this. Nonetheless, I met with the group of strangers, climbed into the van, and settled in to nap through the two-hour ride to Mount Adams. When we reached the trailhead, we got out, stretched, and went along our way. Soon our early awakening and zealous hiking were rewarded. As I rounded a bend in the trail, I encountered an enchanted scene: shafts of sunlight filtered down through the dark canopy, illuminating the white wisps of mist that rose gently from behind a small grey boulder in the middle of the path. Higher up, we passed a picturesque stream and a beautiful waterfall. Then, nearly halfway up the mountain, we came upon a huge boulder that jutted out above the trees. I clambered atop the boulder, strode to the edge, and surveyed the valley below: the trees spread out forever in brilliant shades of red, yellow, and orange; above, puffy white clouds drifted through the intensely blue sky, casting a random cluster of shadows upon the valley below. It was spectacular.

Continuing up the mountain, we scrambled over and slithered under rock formations, leapt crevasses, and circumambulated boulders. As we climbed, the people who had been strangers that morning quickly became friends. When the summit came into sight, we pushed each other ever faster through the last steep scramble to the peak. And then we were there, atop the mountain, looking out at the surrounding peaks, the valley below, and the trail we had just traversed. I felt secluded from the rest of the world; impossibly far from books and classrooms, the mundane details of day-to-day existence. We were on another, brighter, purer level of existence. The experience left me refreshed and invigorated, ready to return to campus and redouble my commitment to my studies.

After that adventure, how could I not go on the next week's trip? And the next? And the next? I ended up hiking almost every weekend, and before long, instead of just participating in trips, I was planning, organizing, and leading them. This is how I became a council member for Cabin and Trail, Dartmouth's hiking and trail maintenance club. With the club, I've climbed the highest peak in New England during a raging blizzard, snowshoed in the middle of winter nights so cold that the world was frozen still. I've learned to repair trails and build cabins, learned wilderness first aid, leadership, and group dynamics skills, and led every kind of trip from a simple walk in the woods, to the complicated, silly, and fabulously fun trip in which we carried a canoe to the top of Mount Washington.

But what is the relevance of my experience with Cabin and Trail? What do hiking and mountains have to do with law? Certainly there is little direct connection between the two. The type of law that I want to practice takes place in the urban locales of Washington, D.C., New York, and Chicago, not the peaks of New England. And knowing the fastest way to build a fire won't improve my ability to write briefs. No, my experience with Cabin and Trail is not what will make me a great lawyer. Rather it is my academic and intellectual qualities, combined with the tenacity and leadership that I have learned from Cabin and Trail, that will make me a great lawyer.

I have learned to develop strong and persuasive arguments by thinking analytically for philosophy papers and debate rounds. I have honed my research and writing skills by writing a thesis about the constitutionality of the detention of U.S. citizens as "enemy combatants." I have learned to adapt quickly to new people, new places, and new practices by studying and traveling throughout the United States and abroad. I have learned to thrive in a professional environment by working in professional, government, and nonprofit organizations. And I have fanned the flames of my passion for law through my study of political theory and constitutional law.

While the skills that I developed with Cabin and Trail are not the skills that will make me a great lawyer, they have fostered traits that will make me a unique lawyer. My experiences in the woods and atop the peaks give me a different perspective than [that of] those students who rarely venture into the wilderness. The confidence and persistence that led me to the tops of the mountains will lead me to accept and succeed at challenges that others shy away from. My experience with unexpected, difficult, and even dangerous situations on the trail will help me keep my cool when unforeseen challenges arise in the courtroom. Guiding groups of strangers through the woods has strengthened my interpersonal skills. The connection with nature has refined my perspective on man's place in the universe. And the love of adventure and sense of humor that Cabin and Trail nurtures give me an indomitable and optimistic attitude that I believe sets me apart from many others. My experience with Cabin and Trail is not what will make me a great lawyer. Rather it is what will set me apart from other great lawyers that I encounter.

Climbing the Mountain

Review by A. Haven Thompson

Eric Benson's essay is a good example of how to show that your experience in an extracurricular activity will translate into success at law school. Benson's careful structure and explicit demonstration of his interest in the law keeps this essay focused and prevents it from collapsing into a collection of musings about the beauty of the wilderness.

Benson's opening, in which he describes his first excursion with Cabin and Trail, could have benefited from the use of more striking language. If he replaced overused adjectives like "picturesque" and "beautiful" with more colorful words, Benson could have breathed some life into the nature that he encounters on his hike.

And yet, Benson's choice to devote the first two paragraphs of his essay to the hike shows how central his outdoor adventuring is to his sense of self. He anticipates that his readers may furrow their brows at the connection he draws between Cabin and Trail and his law school application, and he neatly contrasts the remoteness of his mountain excursions with the urban environments in which he plans to practice law.

This transition allows Benson to explain his passion for the law, as he lists the professional and academic accomplishments that have prepared him for law school. Benson argues that his intellect will intersect with the skills he obtained during his time in Cabin and Trail. This unique combination, he contends, will make him a great lawyer and give him the perspective and leadership experience that other potential students might lack.

If you plan to write your essay on an extracurricular activity, Benson provides a good model to follow: begin by focusing in detail on your extracurricular [activity], and then discuss how it relates to a career in law.

KEVIN BLUM

As the drumroll began and the spotlight centered on the stripper, she flashed the patrons of the Red Rat a teasing smile. From my spot below the stage, I grinned in satisfaction. That brisk evening in March 2005 was not only the opening night of the Case Footlighters production of *Jekyll and Hyde*, but also my conducting debut. After years of performing in pit orchestras, I had finally been asked to direct one. The weeks leading up to the show had been filled with activity, with rehearsals often going until well after midnight. I had put in my fair share of fourteen-hour workdays, in addition to sending out countless e-mails and rearranging works at the last minute. I was directly in charge of conducting the orchestra, so once the curtain went up, everything depended on me. The stage lights turned on when I started the overture; Jekyll became Hyde when I cued the string section; the audience applauded when I released the final chord.

As pit director, it was my responsibility to make sure all those involved were performing their duties perfectly in sync with one another. For example, I had to explain to a lighting specialist without musical training that he had to turn on the spotlight three measures after the timpani started playing. I provided only the information necessary for the specialist to do his job, and explained to him how to watch my conducting pattern so that he could count the measures as a musician would. The task of pulling together an entire musical seemed daunting, especially as I had never acted in, directed, or done technical work for one before. Yet I had the utmost confidence in myself, because this challenge was no different from other challenges I had faced in different contexts. Translating technical information into complete yet simple descriptions is one of my most well developed skills.

My ability to convert complex information into clear and concise explanations extends beyond the arts. This past summer, I participated in the Case Leadership Internship program, which places twelve undergraduates a year in internships exposing them to jobs suited to their interests and skill sets. Due to my economic analysis skills and interest in politics, I was assigned to the James Draper for Mayor of Cleveland Campaign, where, as part of my duties, I collected and analyzed elections data to determine which precincts in the city were the most important ones on which to focus. For each precinct, I took into account such factors as party affiliation, past voter turnout, and past loyalty to incumbents. My finished product was a list of all the precincts in the city, ranked in order of importance. In order to convince the campaign manager, analysts, and coordinators to follow my recommendations, I had to explain my methods and reasoning in succinct terms. I needed to justify my conclusions to volunteers, many of whom did not have any exposure to the statistics of Cleveland politics. My explanations succeeded because I fully understood the material, assumed no prior knowledge, and boiled my explanations down to just a few sentences, so as not to overwhelm. Because of my work, the campaign manager offered me a part-time job as a full-fledged member of the campaign staff once my internship ended in early August. I remained with the campaign until Mr. Draper was defeated in the October primary.

The final chord sounded. The curtain closed on Emma Carew, resplendent in her wedding dress, weeping over the corpse of her fiancé, Dr. Henry Jekyll. The show had been a resounding success; the final evening of the show's run had broken the Footlighters' record for ticket sales. Every member of cast and crew, from actor to ticket taker, had performed his or her part flawlessly. I am proud that my contributions as pit director, especially my explanatory skills, helped to make this a rewarding experience for all.

Review by Adam Goldenberg

This essay is remarkable for being tied together with a simple, yet compelling, narrative yarn. The piece opens with a bang—a colorful image of a stage-strutting stripper gyrating to the cue of Kevin Blum's baton. This serves a double purpose—not only does it grab the reader's attention with a catchy opening, but it also makes clear Kevin's exceptional musical background, which would presumably set him apart from other applicants.

Once the anecdote has been introduced, Kevin makes a smooth transition to articulating his own particular skills, which are applied both to his work as a musical director and to his potential as a law school applicant. "Translating technical information into complete yet simple descriptions is one of my most well developed skills," he writes.

Kevin is also effective because of wise structural choices in his writing. The narrative of his experiences alternates between Kevin's challenges and his responses to those challenges. Kevin presents each of his accomplishments as a hard-to-come-by response to a distinct challenge, be that challenge a tone-deaf lighting operator or a group of campaign volunteers with no statistics knowledge. This distinctly humble posture builds to a sort of punch line; the job offer extended to Kevin by the Draper campaign's manager at the conclusion of his internship speaks highly of Kevin's competence, and is a nice reward for the on-the-job communication and ingenuity that the essay describes. By building up to the job offer this way, Kevin gives the entire paragraph a comfortable finality, lends stylistic weight to his capping achievement, and neatly concludes the passage.

This is a successful essay because Kevin keeps the reader interested with good style points and an involving narrative without losing clarity. A reader will remember not only Kevin's individuality and his specific accomplishments, but also his self-diagnosed talents as an effective communicator.

NIKA ENGBERG

It's not that I'm so smart, it's just that I stay with problems longer.
—Albert Einstein

I walk into the university sports center, through a concrete maze illuminated by fluorescent lights, to a brick-lined corridor with one very unique wall. Twenty-five years old, the wall is dotted with numbered pieces of concrete. Some of them protrude out of the vertical wall while others recede back into it. These concrete features are caked with the chalk that rock climbers use to dry their hands, as well as [with] the high-friction rubber found on the bottom of climbing shoes. This is what has passed for my climbing gym for the last six months. It is the polar opposite of the shiny new facility I train at when I am back at home, but I have come to appreciate its unique challenges.

Today's challenge is literally what climbers call a "problem": a short, specific climbing route that involves moving along the wall using only eight of its 117 holds. Only two people have ever climbed it without falling. If I too succeed, it will be the hardest thing that I, or any other woman, will have climbed at this wall. It is unsurprising, then, that my attention is divided when I greet my crew of friends upon arriving in the dim corridor. My eyes wander above their heads, studying the problem I hope to solve. My fingers twitch and my muscles tense, but I remain calm.

My friends sit along the other side of the corridor to watch my attempt. They hope to see me succeed, and I know that they are preparing to encourage me. This delights me. Although I have already decided exactly how to complete each individual movement the problem requires, methodologically working out my exact body positioning on previous attempts, I know that their cheers will give me added determination to link these moves together into the problem's solution.

Climbers' convention dictates that I begin the problem by pulling myself out of a sitting position on the ground in order to make it more challenging, which I dutifully do. The first move is easy for me, and the second isn't much harder. I'm focused but relaxed. One observer tells another, "This is clearly much more difficult for her than it is for us," as I hop to reach the next hold rather than simply statically touching it the way taller climbers do. Although the hold is only as thick as the edge of a quarter, and my fingertips can barely rest on it, I manage to shift my weight to an exact position that allows me to bring my other hand onto the same hold, just as I have practiced. The two male climbers who have succeeded on this before me claim that this is the most difficult movement required by the problem. However, I have the motion ingrained in my mind and body from previous attempts. As I employ my muscle memory, it feels effortless. For me, the hardest move is yet to come.

My friends know that this next move is where I usually fall off the problem. Once again, I cannot reach a hold that taller climbers can, but [I] have discovered a unique and difficult sequence of hand and foot movements that allows me to arrive at it. This time, I do not fall, and my friends cheer. The crux of the problem is finished. All I have left to complete is the easier final movement. After having tenaciously experimented on this final move to discover the best way to complete it, I have memorized the exact point where I need to balance my toe against the wall in order to succeed. Knowing that I have done the hardest part, I place my toe against the flat wall and reach for the final hold. As I grab it, my foot swings off the wall and I fall. I'm not sure why it happened; maybe I didn't clench my stomach muscles quite tight enough, maybe my toe was a centimeter too high on the wall, maybe my friends caused me to lose concentration rather than contributing to my focus. The problem remains unsolved for me because success requires that I touch the final hold with both hands, rather than simply one.

My friends reassure me, saying that I'm sure to finish this problem

Climbing the Mountain

soon, but I begin to have doubts. Meanwhile, they return to talking and flirting with each other. Some wander to a far end of the wall to continue their work on their own climbing problems. Others remain to discuss their life problems with each other, attempting to solve them. With their backs to me, I resolutely sit back down on the ground to try again. Witness-less, I succeed.

Review by A. Haven Thompson

Engberg begins her essay with a punch, quoting Albert Einstein. An epigraph can be a good way to frame and center your essay, but beware that it may distract the reader if it isn't explicitly pertinent to your essay. In this case, the "problems" that Einstein faced and the "problem" that Engberg tackles are very different. The quotation links them, showing that Engberg's attempt to master a difficult climb parallels her perseverance in her academic and personal life.

The rest of the essay serves as an extended metaphor for Engberg's motivation and work ethic, as she tries and fails, then tries again and succeeds, at a very challenging climbing route. Notice her careful use of detail, which strengthens the essay—she describes features such as the room's fluorescent lighting and the exact number of handholds on the climbing wall. While the description helps the reader envision the setting of Engberg's story, her diction also reveals her attention to detail and knowledge of the sport.

The most masterful part of the essay is the final line. Engberg tells us that she has succeeded at the very end, almost in passing, demonstrating that she derives as much satisfaction from the journey as she does from its final outcome. Engberg does not climb to receive praise from her audience or outside reassurance—her friends, in fact, aren't even paying attention when she finally conquers the "problem." Rather, she dedicates herself to the climb because of her personal desire to succeed.

Engberg is careful not merely to outline accomplishments that admissions officers could read about in her application, such as leadership positions or work experience. Instead, she describes a particular moment that metaphorically conveys the traits of persistence and discipline that she, like the famous physicist from her epigraph, brings to every problem she tackles.

RYAN FRANK

To be honest, I have dreaded this moment for some time. It seems like a daunting task: to write something personal that is meant to engender approval while sounding neither pleading nor arrogant, that will stand out in some way among [the writings] of thousands of other intelligent people striving to achieve the same goal as me, but also avoiding writing anything that will cause the eyes of a probably exhausted reader to glaze over. To possibly make matters worse, I was a theater major in college, and performance is where the bulk of my energies have been directed, leaving a "real world" résumé that is certainly nothing special. I finally realized, though, that I was letting that blind me to the fact that I have managed to make contributions to my community, even if said community was a bit unusual.

When I was working on my bachelor's in theater, the college I was attending was making a concerted effort to draw a greater number of performing arts–oriented students, and I was one of these. This was an exciting time to be there, with a strong feeling of an up-and-coming community, but it did mean that existing organizations and structures were often not quite enough to accommodate a sudden drastic increase in interest.

One of my primary interests as a performer was in improv comedy. I had little experience, but was fascinated by it and wanted to learn everything I could about it. The college did have an extraordinary student improv troupe already, but the sudden increase in interest in

120

acting became a detriment. Once a semester, [there would be] open auditions for new members; usually, up to a hundred people would be competing for one or two slots. This did not leave much of a chance for someone who was not already well trained in this unique genre of performance to join, and [it left] no opportunity to learn and eventually attain that level of proficiency. So, at the beginning of my sophomore year, I decided to make my own opportunity and found my own troupe.

This was a bit of a problem, as I had about as much experience in founding and running organizations as I had in improv. However, I did know how to take advantage of the resources at my disposal. It turned out that an existing organization, the Creative and Performing Arts Community, had the extra funds in its budget and a desire for an ongoing group like mine, so I established my troupe as a subsidiary of [the CPAC, which handled] most of the administrative details. That took care of the structure.

I realized that this could be seen as sour grapes, as an action taken by a rejected auditioner with a grudge, so I took pains to remove any sense of competition with the existing group; after all, my goal was to learn improv, and alienating [the group] would rob my troupe of a potentially valuable resource. I invited the other troupe to see our first show for free in the front row and even went so far as to join their tech crew to establish a connection between the two groups. Student performance groups are highly prone to infighting, and I did everything I could to make sure that did not happen.

There was one last detail, of course; I could set up my own group for those who needed to learn, myself included, but how could I "teach" when the whole point of the group was gaining experience? I saw that I was of limited use as a director with little experience myself, and for my group to succeed I would need someone with more experience to be in charge. I sought out a senior with substantial experience who had long wanted to start such a group, but [who] had never quite gotten around to getting a structure in place. We each had what the other needed. We agreed to share the duties of running the group until auditions were over and the real work was to begin, at which point I turned over full control to him. In the end, everyone got what they wanted; I and several others now had our opportunity to learn and perform, and my partner had the opportunity to close out his college career in charge of his own troupe. Even the first troupe profited, as having a "training camp" improved the quality of the pool of talent from which it could draw. The troupe lasted for several years after the departures of my partner and me, which made me feel that I had made a real contribution to the growth of the performing arts community on campus. The troupe eventually faded away, but the original cast members are all still in very close contact with each other; it is quite the cliché on which to close, but even if they never use what they learned now that they have all graduated, they have still made friendships that look to be lifelong, and I also take pride in having brought them together.

Review by Lois E. Beckett

Ryan starts off on the wrong foot with his rant about how difficult it is to write a personal essay. Everyone knows that it's hard to present yourself in a few paragraphs, and saying so won't set your essay apart. Ryan also relays his nervousness about applying to law school with an undergraduate degree in theater, treating it as a weakness rather than presenting it as a unique merit.

But Ryan uses the rest of the essay to demonstrate that he is perceptive, determined, and more interested in getting something accomplished than feeding his own ego. Rather than trumpeting the fact that he possesses these qualities, Ryan lets readers draw their own conclusions from an account of how he founded his own improv troupe.

Note how he does not get bogged down on irrelevant explanations of why he loves improv or what kind of sketch comedy his troupe specialized in. Instead, he focuses on recounting how he analyzed the problems he found in his college's theater program and how he went about solving them.

At every turn, his narrative highlights his strengths: his positive attitude about getting rejected by the established improv group, his humility about his own inexperience, his determination to learn improv, his planning skills in finding funding for the group, his sophisticated handling of the potential tensions between rival groups. Ryan is especially tactful in his description of the experienced senior partner with whom he created the improv group—he makes it clear that he, not the senior, was the driving force behind the group without blatantly stating that fact.

Ryan follows the "show, don't tell" rule, and it works. He doesn't use sentences like, "This exemplifies how I am both determined and sensitive to other people," and he doesn't need to. He lets his actions speak for themselves. Show admissions officers your good qualities in action rather than listing adjectives in praise of yourself.

TABATHA GEORGE

Among cherished hobbies and interests, I hold particularly dear my ability to make people's heads vanish. I intend this statement in the least metaphorical sense possible, for encroaching blindness has given me superpowers. With a simple redirecting of my blind spots, a stained shirt is rendered clean; a dinner bill is reduced by factors of ten; and a distinguished professor is morphed into a headless body, arms flailing animatedly in an intriguing demonstration of his point. To be sure, blindness is never a dull companion.

I was diagnosed with Stargardt's Disease, a juvenile form of macular degeneration, at seventeen. While I've retained the mobility of a sighted person due to my peripheral eyesight, the fine vision necessary to read books, see street signs, or recognize friends is mostly gone. Though victory despite adversity is often touted as the greatest challenge of a disability, this is the secret about my blindness: fighting is not the hard part. Don't get me wrong; it isn't always easy. My vision often requires more planning and a different approach. But challenge is an irresistible temptress. Edit *Let's Go: Europe* or direct Room 13, then add blindness to the mix—the product is a precious and unique brand of confidence. Much harder than overcoming my limitations is admitting to them. Afraid the elusive line between letting go and giving up would fade with my vision, I spent my first two years of college "passing" for a fully sighted person. I refused to use magnifiers in class, pretended to see things I couldn't, and worked to keep my disability a secret.

Al showed me the peace and strength born of acceptance. Each plain, white door at Chilton House Hospice is adorned with a dry-erase board. His read, "Al: A Friendly Guy." I sat with Al every Sunday for the last four months of his life. One evening, his hand trembled so violently he was unable to hold a fork. I offered to help, and Al accepted. Afterward, he declared, "That was the best dinner I've ever had." Al made this claim after every meal, but this time his words catapulted beyond endearment and landed in the realm of the sublime. I fought tears as my irrational equation of disability and weakness came blissfully crashing to the ground. Al had lost the ability to feed himself, but as he sat back, Lincoln-like in his tall armchair, I had never seen a person look more dignified.

Inspired by Al's courage, I decided it was time to change the way I dealt with my own impairment. In perfect personal-statement splendor, the peak moment of my experience as a blind person occurred on top of a mountain. My junior year of college, I tried blind skiing. The sport involves verbal cues from a sighted guide and orange safety vests. For me, the scariest part of blind skiing was not barreling down a mountain with no usable vision; it was putting on the bright orange vest that said, "Blind Skier." Fiercely independent, I had long feared the day when I would not only have to acknowledge my limitations, but inform those around me of them as well. As I stood at the top of my first ski run since high school, my hands shook, and my large red mittens refused to cooperate with the vest's small fastening hooks. My guide offered his help, and I accepted. It was the first time I was easily identifiable as a blind person, and to my great surprise, the world did not crumble. The sky did not fall. To the contrary, a previously uncharted world of convenience and understanding emerged around me: the chair lift slowed, other skiers kept their distance, and life was easier than it had been in a long time.

I returned to Harvard with the wisdom that acknowledging limitations opens new possibilities. That spring, I cosponsored a fundraiser for the Foundation Fighting Blindness and gave several speeches, including one to the College Council. Marvin Bell writes of losing vision: "Autumnal light/gave to ordinary things the turning/beauty of leaves, rich with their losing."[2] Blindness is indeed a beautiful and enriching loss—the gems of wisdom my shattered vision reveals remain my most treasured life lessons. So, when the daily grind of low vision wears me thin, I imagine a day when I'll go soaring down that mountain once more: I throw my poles behind me, crouch firm against the wind, and shoot a smile to the headless skier next to me. It's a beautiful place to be.

Review by William C. Marra

This is an immensely powerful essay about a person's coming to terms with a disability and overcoming a daunting obstacle in life. Tabatha's essay succeeds not simply because the disability is so

[2]Marvin Bell, *Nightworks, Poems 1962–2000* (Washington: Copper Canyon Press, 2000).

serious, but rather thanks to the richness and detail in her story-telling. Her narration is effective because she describes in great detail what happened and what she did on several moving occasions, while also discussing her mental state throughout these events. She thus engages the reader on two levels, as we follow her physical struggles in life as well as her mental ones. The end of the essay brings it full circle, as the "beautiful place" she finds herself is both a physical and spiritual locale.

If you are writing an essay about overcoming an obstacle of some sort, there is much to be learned from Tabatha's piece. Notice how she creates an arch over the course of the essay, describing and demonstrating what the obstacle is, then discussing the turning point (her meeting with Al), and finally her experience once she overcame the obstacle and was able to go skiing. At the heart of adversity essays should be strong descriptive language that makes the reader feel a part of the action. Your goal is to convey something about the strength and quality of your character, and so you should recall the popular grade-school essay-writing lesson: wherever possible, *show*, do not *tell*, what happened or how you changed and grew as a person.

SUSAN GERSHON

Working in Vermont politics in the summer and fall of 2004 felt a great deal like jumping into a lake with a thorough theoretical background in ocean kayaking to keep me afloat: I knew both far more and far less than I needed, and ultimately found my way with a lot of advice and no small amount of thrashing around.

When I was accepted by the 21st Century Democrats to work on one of their campaigns, I have to admit that I envisioned something a bit different from the situation I found myself in. I was ready to work long campaign hours and to be more outgoing and assertive than is my general habit, but I wasn't entirely prepared for the extent to which I would be on my own.

After a whirlwind three-day training session, I found myself back home in the county where I had grown up, suddenly designated as the entire full-time staff for the thirteen Democrats running for the state legislature from Rutland County. This was not a position I had been expecting nor, since Vermont legislature races are among the smallest in the country, was it precisely what I had been trained for.

In Vermont, the average statehouse campaign is won or lost by three or four hundred votes. The average campaign budget is a bit shy of three thousand dollars, and while the average candidate probably doesn't actually knock on every door . . . , [he or] she certainly tries. To some of these candidates I was simply a representative from the state party. To others I was a volunteer coordinator, mailing strategist, literature designer, media consultant, taskmaster, events planner, debate advisor, or campaign manager. For each campaign I slowly worked out what combination of roles I would play. While I had good support from the state party staff, there was a lot that I had to figure out, and there were many practical and strategic choices I had to make on my own. Frequently I found that I simply did not know, and in some cases couldn't have known, what the right decision was.

That is of course a fairly unremarkable statement. On a theoretical level I was familiar with that kind of uncertainty; in my college papers I often concluded that the answer to the question posed was "yes, however . . ." I spent many pleasant hours contemplating strengths and flaws of a variety of theories without reaching anything so practical as a definitive answer. Still, I think a large part of me felt that that kind of uncertainty ends, or should, at the classroom door, and that in work in the "real world," decisions would be somehow simpler, clearer, and with less room or need for the "however."

As the campaign wore on, I found more "howevers" than I was comfortable with, and had less time for research and contemplation than I was accustomed to. In my job I had to make the call about how to coordinate with other campaigns, where to put volunteers or money, or how best to target a mailing; while there were certainly people I could ask for advice, it was ultimately my responsibility to find the relevant information and decide what to suggest that the candidate do. These decisions were not earth-shattering, but they were important, and having never before held a job or other position with so many decision-making responsibilities, I was often afraid that my choices and suggestions would be the wrong ones. Sometimes I cared so much about getting it right that a part of me wanted to do nothing at all, and settle for at least not getting it wrong. But life marches on [despite] uncertainty, and I learned, and will continue to learn, how to accept that I have to march on with it and do the best I can.

In retrospect, I think I did well for the candidates I worked with, and for the most part I believe that I made the right decisions. I probably made some wrong ones as well. I still think about the sixty votes by which one of my candidates lost, and rehash debates about this kind of event or that kind, this mailing or that one. Still, my life has indeed gone on, and I'm going to keep on making choices, and doing the best I can to gain the knowledge and keep the energy and passion I need to get them as close to right as possible.

Review by Kyle L. K. McAuley

Gershon's essay has enormous unrealized potential and plenty of empty space to explore it. She still holds on to that classroom theorizing she laments, as her essay contains no specific stories or example to illustrate her personal observations. Her prose is engaging and her thoughts flow logically, but [she] does not touch us. Her observations exist in the theoretical world, and they stay there.

Consider the passage, "I was ready to work long campaign hours and to be more outgoing and assertive than is my general habit, but I wasn't entirely prepared for the extent to which I would be on my own." She is *telling* us what she learned and how she adapted, but the sentence comes out empty. As you write your own essay, illustrate and show what you've learned through examples rather than simply stating it. Otherwise, your words will hold little meaning and won't tell your reader much about you.

The problem could have been fixed easily by an extended example or two from her tenure under any one of the Vermont Democrats she campaigned for. Aside from a passing reference to a candidate losing by sixty votes, she shuts the reader out of this supposedly formative experience.

Her essay also does not tell us much about why she is applying to law school, and in fact makes no reference to the actual practice of law. While her experiences may seem interesting, they will not spur an admissions officer to say that she is an excellent applicant. Even if your application and résumé are strong, let your résumé list your activities, and make the most of your essay by communicating something that won't appear anywhere else on your application.

ALEJANDRO MORENO

The dawn of the twenty-first century will present new challenges for those who choose to become tomorrow's lawyers. A paradigm shift from a parochial view to an international perspective of law will become ever more apparent as this century progresses. The integration of world markets and the international homogenization of corporate governance structures demand attorneys who can move seamlessly between different legal and national cultures. As a Mexican American who lived for the first seventeen years of his life in Tijuana, Mexico, I have been able to see the effects of global integration up close. The frenetic pace of life in a bustling border town can appear daunting; however, it also affords the opportunity to live in and be part of one of the vanguards of globalization. During my youth in Tijuana I was able to notice many of the subtle nuances that prevented people from the United States and Mexico from fully comprehending each other. This instilled in me a desire to seek a profession where I could help bridge the gap in understanding that separates these cultures and help both communities to continue to develop economic, artistic, and societal ties.

At the age of seventeen I moved to San Diego to complete my final year of high school. I attended one year of high school in the United States so that I could polish my literacy skills in English as well as prepare for college-level courses. Although I was a native English speaker (learning both languages as a child), I wanted to make sure I would be able to compete in an all-English setting. After graduation from high school I enrolled at the University of California, Santa Barbara. In college I chose political science as my major because of my interest in local, national, and international politics. While at UCSB I was selected for a scholarship to attend a national presidential convention. Furthermore, I was actively involved in the presidential primary of 2000 as the student director of the drive to elect John McCain. In my sophomore year I was elected by my peers to represent them in the Associated Student Council. As a council member, I worked with colleagues to fund student activities centered on leadership, diversity, and other humanistic concerns.

My tenure at UCSB provided me with a remarkable opportunity to further explore my interest in international politics and globalization. I spent my junior year abroad in Barcelona, Spain, and devoted most of my research to understanding the supranational implications of the European Union. My Spanish professors in sociology, international relations, and public service guided this research and provided critical feedback on what became my best paper while abroad. Although writing more than twenty pages, in Spanish, on an innovative subject was a demanding task, earning the respect of my academic peers was worth the effort.

Spain also sharpened my ability to adapt to different cultures and new situations. I developed strong ties with the local Catalan political science students. Apart from being great friends and classmates, these young Catalans allowed me to observe firsthand the divergent trends of regional nationalism and European integration. I also had the privilege to live with a Hungarian, an Israeli, and two German MBA students who each introduced me to his own peculiar way of making sense of the world and absorbing the problems and hopes that bind us. From my stay in Spain, I developed a deep belief that the process of globalization must not erode the distinctive characteristics that set apart each nation's culture.

I would like to end this statement on a personal note that will give the reader a holistic impression of who I am as an individual. My thirst for knowledge branches into many different disciplines and arts. Since childhood I have had a strong affinity to the classics of literature and art of the Greco-Roman world. Whether by studying Polikleitos's seminal sculpture the *Doriphoros* or the stirring epics of Homer, the earthy reality that is presented in these works seems more sincere than much of modern day's mass culture. My interest in literature extends to modern-era classics. A large amount of my free time is devoted to analyzing and digesting the works of James Joyce, Seamus Heaney, Vladimir Nabokov, and García Márquez, among others. The heady sensuousness of modern literature provides a spellbinding escape from modern life's travails. Although I must admit to sometimes being overwhelmed by the amount of progress humanity has achieved in science, I subscribe to *Scientific American* to at least develop a rudimentary grasp of where we are headed as a species. This passion for science extends from the sweeping advances in cosmology and string theory, to the minutiae of how the beaks of Darwin's finches allow us to gain insights into the mechanisms of natural selection. My need for intellectual stimulation is far from satiated. As a law student, I expect that I will have multiple opportunities to continue to explore our world, our systems of beliefs, and our humanity. I will end this essay with a few words from W. B. Yeats.

> *Had I the heavens' embroidered cloths,*
> *Enwrought with golden and silver light,*
> *The blue and the dim and the dark cloths*
> *Of night and light and the half light,*
> *I would spread the cloths under your feet:*
> *But I, being poor, have only my dreams;*
> *I have spread my dreams under your feet;*
> *Tread softly because you tread on my dreams.*[3]

Review by Sam Teller

The writer's opening paragraph succeeds for three reasons: it sets him apart from other applicants by discussing his background; it demonstrates his ability to write clearly; it outlines the core of his personal desire to attend law school. What it does not provide is a compelling reason why the law school should want him. The second paragraph, while informative, does not contribute a great deal besides reviewing his achievements. What it does demonstrate is the writer's ability to assimilate and engage in multicultural proactive work. Indeed, his awareness of multiculturalism is his salient strength. While his emphasis is less explicitly related to law than other essays, this writer demonstrates a personal passion related to law backed up by numerous personal anecdotes that demonstrate his personal perceptiveness and aplomb. Overall, this

[3]W. B. Yeats, *William Butler Yeats: Selected Poems and Four Plays* (New York: Scribner, 1996), 27.

essay's fundamental weakness is a lack of coherence. The writer does not stick to one central theme, and takes a left turn with the last paragraph. He ends weakly, using someone else's words, when the reader most certainly would prefer to hear him speak instead.

VICTORIA SHANNON

I have been called "baby" more times in my life than the ubiquitous addressee of mid-twentieth-century love songs. And the statement was not meant as a compliment to my looks. "You graduated from college and you're only twenty?" "You must be some kind of prodigy child or something." "Doesn't it feel weird to be so young?" "Oh, you're just a *baby*." Age had been the defining factor in my life growing up and had overshadowed most of the other aspects of my identity in the eyes of both my peers and my parents' peers. Despite other people's qualms about the maturity level of someone my age, my parents felt confident in allowing me to attend a three-summer mathematics and science program at a boarding school located over a thousand miles away, beginning [when I was] thirteen. Hence, from a very early age I learned not to let external boundaries and limitations keep me from pursuing goals that I felt I was keen enough and ready to handle.

At sixteen, I knew that I was ready for college, but upon arrival, I soon found that I was not prepared to be an academic. My high-school curriculum had led me to a basic understanding of subjects like mathematics, English, and history, but the goal of college was to learn to think in new ways about these conventional areas of study. For me, the problem became finding the field of inquiry that most suited my interests. [In] freshman year, a curiosity about artificial intelligence led me to struggle through many introductory courses in computer science and neurobiology. [During] sophomore year, I realized that the study of human thought was more my forte, and [I] switched my focus to psychology. Soon afterward, my grades began a gradual upswing. [In] junior year, I enrolled in a scintillating course linking psychology and the legal system by examining the various psychological defenses used in several famous murder trials. I was intrigued by the fact that a situation or piece of evidence could be construed in so many different ways, such as an opportune manifestation of a defendant's mental disorder or evidence of premeditation in a crime of passion. For me, the hook was the thought process rather than the outcome itself. How was the evidence dissected? Along what criteria were the conclusions drawn? Furthermore, what did these conclusions reveal about the underlying biases in the legal system and the motives of its human elements?

This interest in thought processes led me to take further courses dissecting theories of social psychology, but none of these courses intrigued me as much as my course on psychology and law. In the summer after junior year, I found another unique connection between psychology and the law through the field of dispute resolution, which I learned was a means by which an outside individual could convince contending parties to collaborate through an issue-driven thought process. I enrolled in two negotiation courses at Harvard Law School during my senior year, and while the process was arduous, I was determined not to let the perceived boundaries of my undergraduate status limit my access to graduate-level opportunities. I had finally found my field of inquiry, and I was ready to take on the challenge of law coursework.

Outside the classroom, I was taking on the challenge of raising campus awareness of race and gender issues as president of Women in Color (WINC), an organization dedicated to examining facets of race and gender through artistic, political, and social endeavors. The organization began during the summer before my junior year when twelve undergraduate women of various ethnic and cultural backgrounds and I wrote a theatrical presentation exploring the intersection of race and gender. I coined the title "The Women in Color Project" because we were not only women *of* color, but also women charged with bringing monochrome America into the full realization of its own vibrant Technicolor, "Techni-gendered" population. The innovative production gave rise to an organization of the same name. During WINC's second year, I absorbed the position of executive producer into my presidential duties when the producer of our yearly show suddenly had to leave the board. Though I had no experience with the process of production, I knew that in order for the organization to survive past my presidency, I would need to cement the yearly theatrical tradition. I learned as much as I could about production from theater department gurus, and I enjoyed the process of organizing and preparing a team of cast and crew members for such a groundbreaking show. Despite many hardships, WINC's second production succeeded tremendously, and I restructured the constitution to include the position of play coordinator in the list of required board members. Now, WINC members are working on their third production, scheduled for February 2004.

The challenges I have successfully navigated throughout my college career have demonstrated that my young age was not a hindrance to my maturity, as others had thought. When there was no campus organization addressing issues of race and gender, I started one and ensured its stability through its toughest year. When the undergraduate curriculum did not cover my area of interest, I took the steps necessary to enroll in graduate courses that did, and worked diligently to prove that I deserved my place in them. Now, I want to learn how to best combine dispute resolution and conventional litigation from the scholars who teach and refine both processes. Having taken two law courses, I know that I will be able to adjust to the demanding workload and rigorous environment. Not only will I be a diligent law student, but I also have the drive to start new organizations, incite new discussions, and carve new academic and professional pathways on your campus.

55 Successful Harvard Law School Application Essays

Review by Sahil K. Mathani

This essay reads like an extended commentary on Victoria's résumé. It conveys her precocious engagement with legal issues in her academic work and her involvement in a theatrical production on race and gender. It is particularly effective at conveying the mentality behind each novel academic interest, even if it is at times redundant with her résumé (as when she summarizes WINC's functions).

Even if it is at times unclear why Victoria was so intrigued by a particular field, a sense of genuine academic curiosity is effectively conveyed to the reader. Rhetorical questions, oftentimes the millstones of a sharp argument, here work to Victoria's advantage; they evidence a real interest in the details of her discipline. Because her sentences end in question marks rather than periods, they indicate that her quest for knowledge is unfinished—hence her application to Harvard Law School.

One of the essay's weaknesses is its excessive emphasis on hierarchy. Her transition from the position of executive producer to president; her emphasis on her youth or lack thereof; her selection of law school classes as an undergraduate; her focus on grades—all this suggests a very driven and motivated person, but to what end? An excellent and well-managed dramatic production, but what was it actually about? An interest in psychology, yes, but for what purpose? By the end of this essay, we are still unaware of Victoria's worldview, of what makes her tick.

Still, as you write your own essay, there is much to learn from Victoria, not the least of which lies in her expressive language. Note especially the flair in her first paragraph, which introduces a confident and self-aware narrator. If you begin with a strong introduction that tells your reader that you are an interesting person who will have something valuable to say, you will have succeeded in piquing interest in your essay, and your application.

EMILY WITTEN

I am as far from the classroom as I could have ever imagined. At 6:15 on a Wednesday morning, I am standing in the orange glow of humming sodium vapor lamps, in the middle of tense negotiations with my foreman over the precise meaning of the word "install." The stakes riding on this discussion are high. If the task is determined to be outside the contract, it will cost me. Mud seeps through the eyelets of my steel-toed boots as I point to the appropriate section of the inch-thick contract. After eight minutes of grim bargaining, we conclude that I will pay for the stainless-steel tubing and two hours of a welder's time, and he will finish the rest of the job. No one mentioned in engineering school that the most valuable skills to have are a hair-splitting grasp on the finest details of a contract and the ability to haggle shamelessly like a used-car salesman.

This is my special talent—I speak "engineer." Most people don't understand what engineers love talking about, and for the most part, engineers aren't the best equipped to explain it to them. I can speak both languages, technical and nontechnical. My job at EDM Services, an engineering consulting firm, is to produce information rather than a product. In my two years here, I have produced more than thirty-six bookshelf inches of reports. In order for the customer to be satisfied, I must write clearly and concisely to explain complex technical topics in a way that my customers, often nontechnical managers, can understand. I have to be able to communicate and negotiate with a variety of people—scientists, engineers, upper-level management, and construction workers who may not even have a high-school education.

I had been out of engineering school for only one year when I was put in charge of a $3.5-million pipeline construction project, over five hundred miles from my office. When a crisis arose at 7 A.M., an hour before anyone at my company arrived at the office, I was the only one there to address the problem. Engineering school had taught me a lot of math, but it hadn't taught me how to manage a project. I had been plunged into a completely new world. The only people I could ask for advice were not necessarily on my side. My contractor was the most experienced with construction methods, but I had to take his recommendations with a grain of salt. He was also interested in padding his profit with expensive "extras." My inspector was knowledgeable about rules and regulations, but he was skeptical of anything that wasn't being done his way. My boss, far away at the home office, couldn't solve every problem via cell phone. I learned to consult many sources and then use my best judgment to make the final decision.

I am a confident and assertive person. These personality traits made the construction workers take me, a young woman, seriously. The biggest lesson I had to learn on this project was to focus on listening, rather than talking. I have an opinion about everything, and I always jump right into any discussion with something to say. On this project, I didn't know all the answers. I had to learn each person's skills and personality traits to be able to manage the project's quality and cost. Surprisingly, being promoted to project manager taught me more about listening carefully than about giving orders.

Start-up day finally arrives. Everyone has butterflies in his (her!) stomach. At noon, natural gas must flow through the new line to be delivered to the refinery. Refinery operations have already been shut down for a week, at a cost of $20,000 per day, to allow us to tie the new pipeline into the system. Start-up must proceed on schedule, and gas must be delivered today. The control panel in Houston begins to pressure up the system. When the gauges read 485 psi, gas begins to flow into the refinery. We all hold our breath. Even one poorly installed gasket could cause a dangerous explosion. The call comes in—everything is working perfectly. The thousands of decisions, man-hours, and mechanical parts that made up this pipeline project had received the only acceptable passing grade—100 percent.

Climbing the Mountain

Review by April Yee

If the point of an essay is to make the reader feel he knows the writer, then Emily has earned herself an A. After reading this, the reader knows what she once wore (steel-toed boots), who she is (a woman in a man's world), and what she speaks ("engineer"). She's not just a candidate for law school. She's a vivid writer.

By not revealing that she is a woman until the penultimate paragraph, she surprises the reader without hitting him [or her] over the head. Still, she can't resist adding the parenthetical to the sentence, "Everyone has butterflies in his (her!) stomach."

Her essay could work as convincingly for a job application as one for law school. In her second sentence, she writes how she argues with her foreman "over the precise meaning of the word 'install,'" much as a lawyer might handle negotiations. "I must write clearly and concisely to explain complex technical topics in a way that my customers, often nontechnical managers, can understand," she writes.

The direct language she uses in her essay demonstrates her skills at communicating. She uses words like "haggle," "humming," and "grim." The longest word she uses is "recommendations." Her ability to use simple words to convey a complicated story is one of the best recommendations she can give herself. Unlike other applicants, she shows that she can communicate with the elite and with "construction workers who may not even have a high-school education."

As you write your own essay, strive to speak directly to your reader in the same straightforward, conversational way that Emily does. Use descriptive adjectives and particular anecdotes to illustrate your character, and aim, as Emily masterfully does, to make your reader feel as if they have just spent ten minutes speaking with you rather than reading a piece of paper.

AN INTELLECTUAL DESIRE

KRISTIN BATEMAN

If you had told me two years ago that I would develop a passion for tax policy, I would have said you were crazy. I focused my energies on the lofty ideals of human rights and equality—and left topics such as tax policy to folks wonkier than I.

In college, my dedication to human rights led me to courses on constitutional and international human rights law, courses that introduced me to a way of thought that inspired my interest in a legal career. I delighted in reading different cases, deriving the generally applicable rules, and applying them to hypothetical situations with new sets of nuances. Attracted to such intellectual challenges, I searched for a job where I could merge my desire to gain a "real-world" context for my future legal studies with such human rights issues as a woman's right to choose, religious liberty, and full equality for gay Americans.

I found the ideal position on the Public Policy staff of People for the American Way (PFAW), a nonprofit political advocacy organization known for its work on the very social issues that fueled my political interest. Here, my passions unexpectedly shifted focus.

The technicalities of a relatively minor legislative battle far less sexy than partial-birth abortion and gay marriage sparked my interest in tax policy a mere three weeks into my employment. In May of 2003, Congress excluded nearly seven million low-income families from a widely touted increase in the Child Tax Credit. While this offended my sense of justice, it was what followed that triggered the interest in tax policy that has stayed with me ever since.

In response to this exclusion, the Senate overwhelmingly passed a bill that would extend this tax benefit to these families at no net cost to the Treasury. Whip counts showed that the Senate-passed bill would easily pass in the House as well, but the House Rules Committee prevented *that* bill from reaching the floor and instead offered an expensive bill that had no chance of passing the deficit-conscious Senate. The disdain for open and honest debate exhibited by this parliamentary maneuver appalled me. Millions of working families would not get their tax credit, but members of the House could plausibly, if duplicitously, claim to have cast a compassionate vote.

Hooked, I eagerly accepted an assignment to work on tax issues through Fair Taxes for All, a coalition of over three hundred organizations, including PFAW, major labor unions, religious groups, and social justice organizations. As I immersed myself in the politics and technical details of tax and budget legislation, I discovered an arena where politicians routinely employed parliamentary shenanigans and budgetary gimmicks to mislead the public about the meaning of votes and the costs and trade-offs of policies. Bills that included artificial expiration dates to hide tax cuts' likely costs and procedural tricks that removed the possibility for bipartisan compromise challenged my conception of ethical public policy making and shattered my youthful naiveté. While the revenue-draining and regressive effects of the policies I studied troubled me, I was most disturbed that the policies often relied on arcane details to obscure the real agenda from the public.

These arcane details reinforced my desire to become a lawyer. Crafted—and deciphered—by lawyers, these details have profound implications for the distribution of wealth, the overall health of the economy, and our society's ability to fund public services like education and health care. I have reveled in exposing the significance of this "small print" in action alerts, press releases, and editorial memoranda I have written for the Fair Taxes for All coalition; now I want to be able to tackle these details directly. The complexity of the tax code—along with its requirement of an interdisciplinary approach combining public policy with economics, sociology, and political philosophy—presents an intellectual challenge that entices me. More importantly, I have realized that, by focusing on taxes, I not only promote the public's interests in an underscrutinized arena, I also make an indirect contribution to all the human rights areas on which I have worked.

Indeed, my experiences advocating for prisoners' rights, lobbying for reproductive rights, and protecting voters' rights have convinced me that the law could provide much stronger human rights guarantees, but I now more fully appreciate the critical role that tax and budget policy can play in promoting these rights. While laws restricting inmates' access to the courts and precedents establishing high barriers to proving Eighth Amendment violations frustrated my attempts to improve conditions at a D.C. jail, many of the conditions inmates complained about—poor medical care, lack of access to programs, cell blocks with no heat—resulted from a lack of resources. While the Partial Birth Abortion Ban limits women's medical options (or would if it were not enjoined), recently passed tax cuts redistribute society's wealth in a way that disproportionately disadvantages women and drains federal coffers of revenue that could go to public programs, like child care or comprehensive reproductive health care, that could significantly advance women's emancipation. While many voters were disenfranchised by the application of provisional ballot laws and by malicious voter-suppression efforts, many more lost their vote because states did not have the funds to hire enough elections officials or to buy enough voting machines to serve the voting population. The tax proposals I have encountered over the past year and a half threaten our ability ever to make such investments.

I never thought I would be as excited by an Intro to Tax Law course as I would by Constitutional Law, but my time inside the Beltway has introduced me to the profound role that tax policy can play in promoting the values underlying my attraction to public affairs. Moreover, my work in this area has underscored the intellectual component of the law that draws me to a legal career: as the Supreme Court decisions I read in my college government courses turned on the finest nuances, the construction of law requires attention to the smallest details in order to achieve the grandest goals. I look forward to studying the law and further enriching my understanding of the ways in which tax and budget law, as well as other areas of the law currently unknown to me, permit and constrain individual freedoms and shape possibilities for equality and social justice. And I look forward to using that knowledge creatively to promote human rights.

Review by Daniel J. T. Schuker

This essay offers a model of an effective introduction: in the first two sentences, the author clearly and succinctly tells us what we should expect to read in the other eight paragraphs. And she does it with a buoyancy that draws us in—even if the essay centers on her love of tax policy.

The author uses that unusual passion to distinguish herself from the hundreds of other Harvard Law applicants. A seemingly mundane topic like tax policy, she contends, is in fact intimately bound up with the "lofty ideals of human rights and equality" that many aspiring law students discuss in their application essays. She points us toward a specific interest of hers, and she gives us a concrete subject to grasp from the outset.

But the author also makes clear in her introduction that she is no mere policy wonk. Before proceeding any further, she offers evidence to substantiate her dedication to and passion for the "intellectual challenges" of human rights work. Beyond her general interest in human rights, she says explicitly which areas interest her most: "a woman's right to choose, religious liberty, and full equality for gay Americans."

Finally, she is sure to answer a crucial question facing the admissions officers reading her essay: why does this applicant need to go to law school to cultivate her interests and advance her career? She tells us directly why the "arcane details" of tax policy have made her want to become a lawyer. "Crafted—and deciphered—by lawyers," she writes, "these details have profound implications for the distribution of wealth, the overall health of the economy, and our society's ability to fund public services like education and health care." And she suggests not only why she wants to be a lawyer, but also why she would be a *good* lawyer: she is highly attentive to detail, even "arcane" detail, yet she appreciates the profundity of supposedly dull issues like tax policy. As she writes in her conclusion, "the construction of law requires attention to the smallest details in order to achieve the grandest goals."

And if we read her opening carefully, we could begin to see it all in those first two sentences.

JOHN ENGEL

Accelerated Greek was the most difficult two-course sequence I have ever taken. I spent countless nights memorizing vocabulary and rereading passages in a strange alphabet, often pausing to pore over thick reference books. I studied until my mind was pudding, and studied some more.

In high school I had little interest in literature or art, and I saw nothing but the utilitarian value of foreign languages. Mathematics and science seemed far more serious. A philosophy class I took at the University of Washington before college had sparked a deep interest in that field as well. It seemed clear that cold analysis with logical rigor comprised the only way to approach important questions.

My freshman year I took a required Honors College seminar class on the great works of Western thought. It was entitled "The Human Event," which I think overly broad, but it certainly was an event for me. Over the course of a year we covered ancient through postmodern works. Along the way the professor showed how each work connected to the others. He walked us through close readings of poetry, especially the nineteenth-century Romantics, his specialty. The enthusiasm he felt soon filled me as well.

I noticed that nearly all of the works we read were inspired to some degree by earlier authors. Milton looked back to Dante, who looked back to Virgil, who looked back to Homer. Each author built on the work of all who had come before him. In particular, classical thought and language permeated the required readings, even into the nineteenth and twentieth centuries. I remember my surprise at finding Thoreau's prose sprinkled with classical quotations and allusions, and I found it extraordinary that someone so far removed in time and space from the ancient world would value its literary culture so strongly. At the end of the course I decided to learn a classical language. I wanted a deeper understanding of these authors, and to gain something of lasting value in my undergraduate years. A year and a half later I was immersed in the study of Greek.

My final year at the University of Washington I strongly considered applying to law schools. But I decided that entering a professional program would be rash without a few years of experience in a full-time work environment. Also, I had little knowledge of business, which plays such a large role in our society and in law in particular.

I applied for jobs, but found nothing that suited my goals. So I returned to academia to take a second bachelor's degree in a business-related subject. I learned more about business in my accounting classes than in others, so I majored in the subject. The challenge of the program attracted me as well. Corporate taxation is no pushover.

My experience working over the last twelve months has only strengthened my desire to pursue a legal career. In my philosophy classes I discovered a love of forensic analysis. This brought about my original interest in a legal career and remains my primary motivation. Through work I found that I enjoy working with others in a professional environment toward a common goal. A legal career would be an excellent match with my inclinations and abilities.

I believe my intellectual curiosity and love of challenge will serve me well in my legal career. I focus hard on a subject and have enjoyed every field I have studied. My experience in business will be an asset as well. I have worked in a demanding full-time office environment, and I have gained skills that cannot be taught in a classroom. Harvard Law School, with its substantial resources and strong reputation, would be an excellent place to begin.

Review by William C. Marra

In this essay, John does well to convey his passion for learning across a range of disciplines, including literature, economics, philosophy, languages, and the law. He tracks the development of these intellectual traits from high school, bringing the reader along for the ride. The essay is most compelling at the beginning, where John is able to convey a sense of enthusiasm and excitement as he discovers the language and ancient texts of Greece. His language is filled with action, and we get the impression that he is actively involved and engaged with his education.

The essay slows down in the latter half, and John shifts from the *excitement* of studying Greek to the *difficulty* in studying economics. But what it lacks in animation it makes up for in academic quality. He is appealing to law-school admissions officers because he has a very well-rounded, diverse educational background, which will allow him to apply the law in many different areas of life.

What the essay lacks, however, is a compelling thesis. John's argument here is that he is a very intelligent, educated student. But he could do better by stringing together these diverse experiences and drawing out a more profound lesson that would include but also extend beyond the academic world. His last paragraph applies his skills to law school, but does little to give us any sense of how they transfer over to a legal career, or into what type of lawyer John will be.

MIKE LOQUERCIO

It's almost impossible to encapsulate any dynamic entity with a single word, description, or characteristic. The struggle to define oneself is no exception, so instead of focusing on a single aspect of my overall character, I think an examination of a few themes that persist across many aspects paints a clearer picture.

In many ways, you can truly learn about a person only when you determine how he or she deals with the challenges of life. The behavior is even more telling when someone seeks out these challenges, as I seem to. While applying for an undergraduate education, I was faced with a decision between an upscale university that offered great academic challenge and opportunity with a fairly huge price tag, and a smaller school with less of a name and reputation, yet accompanied by a full scholarship and stipend. Though the decision to be a small fish swimming in a big pond left me in the waters of deeper debt, I feel that the struggles I've had to face as a result of my choice have given me an intellectual and social maturity beyond what I would have otherwise attained. Following my decision to attend Northwestern University, I had to choose whether to stay in their honors program in engineering and law with a guarantee of admission to Northwestern Law School or to transfer into Northwestern's Mathematical Methods in the Social Sciences (MMSS) program and study economics. In following the latter course, I may have made my future a little less secure, but I did get the chance to study something that I found truly intriguing, along with experiences that have brought me much closer to the position I wanted to be in after four years. My pursuit of barriers to overcome continued in my third year at Northwestern when I chose to study abroad in a program with classes taught in Italian by Italian professors. Studying in a completely different academic atmosphere and linguistic world started as a struggle but ended as a unique means of proving my ability to adapt to demanding situations and develop new perspectives. My penchant for seeking out challenges endures in my current decision to follow my original dream of applying to law school rather than seeking employment in the banking or consulting fields like so many of my peers in MMSS.

Part of what has propelled me through the challenges I chose to undertake is the intensity and dedication I bring to my academic endeavors as well as the other facets of my life. Perhaps the best example of this is my dedication to improving myself physically. Though not a natural athlete, perseverance in athletic and mental training allowed me to become an all-conference athlete in high school. Currently, I go to the gym to run or lift weights almost as regularly as anyone I know or have seen there, and [I] have become a valued member of Northwestern's rugby football club. In my experience, it is easier to maintain a healthy and active mind if one also keeps a healthy and active body. I also firmly believe in the doctrine of self-improvement, partly out of a continual desire to face the challenge of bettering myself and partly because I feel that with only a limited time to do so, we should always strive to be the best we can be. This is why I have always sought to challenge myself and those around me and why I will try to continue to do so.

Another pervasive theme of my story that drives, yet at times hinders, the aforementioned trends is my inquisitive and contemplative nature. I constantly question myself and the world around me. I see the world as more interesting because of the because. I am fascinated by how and why things happen, from the technology of the computer I'm typing on—to the physiology of the hands I'm using to do it—to the workings of the mind that drive the whole scenario and especially the society one lives in. At times, my tendency to question myself—my motives, goals, and thought processes—has led me to be indecisive and capricious. Truly, the thinking man is often the last to act. But the ability to intellectually question ourselves and others is what makes us human and what drives our growth as individuals and as a race. This is definitely the case for me individually, as my questioning nature is a major reason why I am who I am today, and at the very least, I'm proud of that.

As I seek admission to Harvard Law School, I am preparing to undertake one of the greater challenges I will have had the prospect of facing. I hope to embrace the opportunity with the same intensity of character with which I approach all things I do, and to glean all I can from a community of academically like-minded but experientially diverse individuals.

Review by Melissa Quino McCreery

Mike's essay reveals a number of attractive qualities—a love of challenges, self-discipline, and inquisitiveness. His writing is at its strongest where he lets his experiences speak for themselves, showing rather than telling us about his character strengths. His decision to choose the MMSS program over engineering and law is a particularly good example of this, as it demonstrates his willingness to pursue his passions while also indicating that law school has been an interest of his for some time.

As you write your own essay, remember that concrete examples carry more weight than abstract assertions. When Mike argues that he brings "intensity and dedication" to his athletic training, his membership on the rugby [football] team is much more meaningful than the claim that he goes "to the gym to run or lift weights almost as regularly as anyone I know." Belonging to a team indicates an understood level of commitment, whereas going to the gym "as regularly as anyone I know" could be a statement as much about the people Mike knows as about his dedication. The best examples are factual and anecdotal—such as "I play rugby" or "I was an all-conference athlete in high school"—rather than subjective assertions.

The essay's greatest weakness is that its language is often unnecessarily convoluted. Sophisticated sentences can be effective, but they lose their impact when they are sandwiched back to back. For example, in explaining why he chose Northwestern and MMSS, Mike's long sentences obscure his reasoning. An essay should look to impress with its content and clarity, not its vocabulary, stylistic flourishes, or complexity. Don't feel as if you have to impress your reader with long sentences or big words—you will find that some of your best sentences will be the short and sweet ones.

DOUGLAS McCLURE

In the first lecture of an introductory philosophy course I took last spring, the professor described some of the questions addressed by philosophers as those that other fields of study raise but fail to address. As a physics concentrator, I had chosen my field of study in part because of my belief in the ability of scientific inquiry to provide definite answers to many of the world's most complex and important questions. In studying physics and participating in research over the last few years, however, I have discovered that the questions I find most compelling are precisely those that scientific research raises but fails to address. Specifically, as developments in the sciences expand the realm of the possible at an increasing rate, they generate ever more complex questions concerning how our laws ought to evolve in response.

Although the study of science has led to technological innovations for many centuries, current research is particularly exciting because across the disciplines of biology, chemistry, and physics, researchers are learning to control the behavior of matter at the most fundamental levels. Many current research efforts in physics, for example, share the goal of exploiting quantum-mechanical phenomena for tasks such as computing and communication. It is difficult at this point to estimate the full range of applications for such technologies, but as an example of the potential increase in computing power, it is predicted that a quantum computer should in a matter of minutes be able to factor numbers so large that the amount of time it would take today's super-computers to perform the same task is longer than the age of the universe. Learning about such research for the first time at a colloquium talk a few years ago, I was fascinated by these possibilities, and I have continued to study them in my classes and lab research.

As I have learned more about such research efforts, however, I have also had the chance to reflect on their broader implications. While a quantum computer able to factor extremely large numbers efficiently would be of great inherent interest to scientists and mathematicians, for example, it would also be of great practical interest to hackers hoping to defeat current encryption technologies used for secure Internet communications. On the other hand, quantum communication technologies may eventually be able to provide a new form of cryptography, allowing completely secure communication. While these sorts of developments will likely necessitate new laws concerning privacy and security, other developments, especially in medicine, may be even more controversial. Indeed, research on stem cells and genetic engineering has already led to questions regarding the extent to which it is in our society's best interest to pursue such research. Advances in engineering may soon lead to new approaches to medicine such as the use of ingestible nanoscale devices to treat and monitor certain conditions. Because their unintentional misuse or deliberate abuse could easily threaten the health of entire populations, however, the availability of such powerful techniques will likely necessitate the careful construction of laws to regulate their use.

An Intellectual Desire

Review by Rachel Banks

McClure's essay treads on the risky ground of controversial topics, but the author is deft at both maneuvering in an inoffensive manner and getting across why he desires to go to law school.

The essay introduces the author's passion for science, raises broad security questions, and provides a solution for the harmful effects of technology. This broad focus is held intact by the author's to-the-point writing style and his succinct yet thorough discussion of the scientific and legal connection. Rather than getting lost in the larger-than-life issues, he considers each of them carefully, makes a conclusion, and leaves the reader with a greater understanding of why the author wants to pursue a career in the legal field.

The topic the author has chosen allows him to set himself apart by discussing his unique, non–pre-law background and how it connects to law. It would strengthen the essay, perhaps, if the author wove more of his philosophical awakenings into the later passages. . . . But by raising such pertinent concerns as Internet security and stem cell research, he ably supports his thesis of wanting to apply scientific knowledge to the legal arena. In doing so, he proves that not only can he handle the challenging thinking that this science major required of him, but that he has the mind for legal challenges as well.

While the author's writing at times may seem science-heavy, he successfully proves that his study of physics has led him to consider the pervasive and potentially destructive nature of science through law—all in a compelling and unbiased fashion.

JANE MORRIL

J. M. Barrie, the author of *Peter Pan*, was, like his fictional character, forever a child. When he was little, he watched his brother die in a skating accident and listened incessantly to his mother's yearnings for her other son—every time [Barrie] would enter the room, she would confuse him with his brother, and then upon realizing who it was, say, "Oh, it's only you." Her only solace was that her son had died as a child, so she could forever retain the image of his youth. Under the severe psychological stress of having his mother ignore him, and under the belief that if perhaps he, like his brother, remained a child, his body stopped producing growth hormones.

I was riveted as Robert Sapolsky, a professor of biology and neuroscience at Stanford, explained how severe stress of the mind can actually affect the way the body functions. I was fascinated by this story because it was the first time I realized how much the mind and body can interact to affect human behavior. While I have always been intrigued by the causes of behavior, until this date I had believed that one could only study behavior from a specific perspective—psychologists studied how the mind and, more specifically, experience affect behavior, while biologists studied how our physical makeup, or our genes, dictates behavior. I felt torn between the two worlds, and was thrilled to learn that human biology was a Stanford major that would allow me to examine the root causes of behavior from an interdisciplinary approach to give me a fuller understanding of why exactly humans behave the way they do.

Indeed, my desire to gain a fuller understanding of human behavior has been the common thread that ties together all of my experiences. During my junior year, I spent a quarter in Washington, D.C., as an intern at the National Institute of Mental Health (NIMH). As an intern at NIMH, I worked with leading scientists and psychiatrists from around the country to develop a strategic plan to assess the current knowledge base of mood disorders and determine areas that needed more research, and thus more funding. In the process, I learned about the causes of mood disorders such as bipolar and, in turn, was able to combine this knowledge with what I had learned at Stanford to help direct mental illness policy.

My understanding of mental illness would not have been complete had I not also had experience in direct public service. Indeed, volunteering at the geropsychiatric center at the Menlo Park Veterans Hospital gave me a more human picture of what it really means to have a mental illness. Spending time with Helen, a bipolar schizophrenic woman in her early eighties, was one of the most difficult experiences I have ever had. Indeed, even after two years of working with her, I could barely get her to acknowledge my presence—during many of my visits she would not even speak to me. But as I continued to visit her, I began to understand how to get her to interact with the other patients, and even found little ways to make her happy, such as playing board games. Without this experience, I would have understood diseases such as bipolar only from a theoretical level—working with Helen forced me to see how these diseases affect real people. I believe everyone in policy [making] should be forced to interact with the people their policies are going to affect.

Even my nonscience jobs have contributed to my understanding of how human behavior works. In my position at Senator [Hillary] Clinton's office, understanding the behavior of her constituents was an important aspect of developing policy within her office. At the district attorney's office, an essential aspect of working in white-collar crime is understanding defendants on a psychological level. In my work on the Tyco case, we have tried to get a fuller picture of what would motivate the defendants to take money from the very company they are designated to run—the key to understanding such motivation is to get a picture of their mental state at the time of the criminal activity. Furthermore, as the trial sets to begin, we, as a trial team, must consider the behavior of our potential jury. Understanding how we want the jury to behave will determine not only what questions we ask them during *voir dire*, but will also determine the direction of our case, and part of knowing how they behave is understanding what causes humans to behave the way they do.

Just as science seeks to understand behavior, law seeks to improve it. I have not merely sought to understand behavior for its own sake—I have always hoped to use this knowledge to somehow improve the world around me. Everything I have done has not only been about understanding behavior, but about helping people while learning. I believe so much in public service that I started a program, modeled after Princeton Project 55, to encourage Stanford seniors to seek jobs in public service by offering three one-year fellowships. I got inspired to start this program after my own frustration at trying to find a job in public service. After working closely with both Princeton and Stanford to implement the program, as well as finding other interested alumni, the fellowship program will begin this year.

Law school will allow me to use my understanding of human behavior to work in both a direct service position, and in a more policy-making function, as I do now at the DA's office. After law school, I will continue to try to apply what I learn in the classroom to the world around me. Only now do I fully realize the importance of hands-on experience in addition to theory—I can honestly say that I have learned more about stress by working at the DA's office than I ever did in the classroom.

Review by Adam Goldenberg

Leading with *Peter Pan* on a law school application is anything but a sure thing. But in this essay, Morril's risky punch is enough to pique the interest of even the most fatigued admissions officer. By making the reader sit up and take notice, Morril increases her chances of being remembered.

Having made a very interesting connection between J. M. Barrie's fiction and the writer's own academic background, the writer lays out in plain and simple language exactly what the "common thread" of her experiences is—in this case, her overarching desire to better understand human behavior.

Morril uses the power of anecdote to its potential in describing her experience working with psychiatric patients. A reader can't help but be compelled by her narrative about Helen, the elderly bipolar woman for whom she cared while volunteering. Morril uses this example not only to illustrate the depth of her scientific interest and qualifications, but also to indicate her commitment to community service.

Morril doesn't forget to mention her legal credentials. In describing her jobs at the Senate and the DA's office, she skillfully maintains her focus, never deviating from her theme of scientific interest in human behavior.

This essay comes together when Morril definitively connects behavioral science and the law. She writes that "just as science seeks to understand behavior, law seeks to improve it." It becomes evident that Morril's scientific experiences and interests are more than a differentiator to set her apart from other applicants—they are the germ for her entire application.

HILARY ROBINSON

I would like to begin by briefly recounting a personal history that has both motivated and inspired me in all of my academic pursuits thus far. In the early 1970s, my father lived and worked for a number of years in East Africa while conducting research on the effects of secondary and postsecondary education in urbanized tribal areas. Then a Ph.D. candidate at the University of Syracuse, his project was jointly sponsored by the university and the Peace Corps and culminated in a comprehensive paper on the subject. Returning to the States to become professor of urban studies and associate dean at the

University of the District of Columbia, my father undertook the very first citywide count of all the homeless on the streets of our nation's capital. His unprecedented analysis and statistical results revealed a population of "hidden homeless" so large as to stun the residents of the city and politicians alike. The methodology he developed for this study was in fact utilized in the most recent national census. In addition to teaching, my father directed an annual seat-belt utilization count in Washington, which promoted the use of these lifesaving restraints and enabled the District of Columbia to share in the benefits of the federal transportation funds. I was only in early adolescence when my father died of cancer in 1994, and since beginning my own academic experience I have come to know him in the past years [through] hearing of these projects and reading his papers. His pursuits and accomplishments have grown to heroic and admirable proportions in my own eyes, but by all accounts he was held in high esteem for his work toward social justice. It is his steps I hoped to retrace during my college years and beyond, for it was my father and ever-strong mother who gave me my interest in learning, my commitment to society, and my biraciality—a perspective that I often realize is unique. I want to continue to strive for their values and for mine, given the tools of a good education and the perspective of coming into adulthood.

Early in my undergraduate years, I became convinced that there existed a pervasive lack of interdisciplinary communication between the fields of natural science and the social sciences or humanities. Entering Harvard, I was consumed by one issue in particular that I felt demanded not only the bridging of academic disciplines, but also international boundaries and ethical schools of thought. This was, of course, the genetic "revolution." As a young college student, my attention was fixed on the most publicized issues: cloning, genetically modified foods, and the compilation of DNA databases. I was especially intrigued by the issues that were most ethically complex: the selection of physical traits, the potential for genetic discrimination, and the patentability of life. I was also fascinated by the issues that continue to be the subject of international controversy: trade in genetically modified crops, biopharmaceuticals, and advances in the science of forensics. I was firmly (and remain) convinced that the age of genetics would be a time of upheaval that could only be moderated through an amalgamation of the efforts of academicians, diplomats, policy makers, ethicists, medical doctors, lawyers, and countless others.

I believe that the difficulty in generating the needed cross-disciplinary discourse stems from a prevailing notion in science: that it is an objective branch of learning where empirical observations result in authoritative knowledge, and into which the equivocating humanities should not intrude. Recognizing this, I petitioned a committee of the faculty of Harvard College to be allowed to pursue a "special concentrations" course of study charted through *both* the social and the natural science disciplines. Believing that there is indeed a subjective and socially constructed side to the study of science, one that can be pinpointed only by joining up with the discipline itself, I proposed to do just that and engage the questions posed when science is considered through a social science lens. Intermediates are necessary to bridge the disciplines and foster dialogue, and I greatly desired to become such a person: the individual with a social awareness, a technological and scientific capability, and a moral and ethical sensitivity. Because the scientific complexities of the new biotechnology are inseparable from an evaluation of their ethical or humanitarian merits, my undergraduate coursework necessarily involved the scientific study of the fundamentals of molecular biology and its medical applications. In tandem with my scientific studies, I continued coursework in government and public policy which encompassed foundational political theory, contemporary policy making, and economics. Furthermore, coursework in social studies, sociology, and the history of science allowed me to focus conceptually on the relationship between science and culture evident in the historical intersections of technology and society.

It has been a challenging undergraduate journey; one in which many fellow students have raised their eyebrows at the student of government who found herself at the microscope, and likewise at the scientist who came to discuss the nature of human reproductive desire with a class of sociologists. Despite encountering a good deal of skepticism, realizing that the lens of one discipline often casts a heated beam onto the discipline being observed, I have continued to drive toward my goal of assisting in the process of understanding and harnessing the genetic revolution. My recent work for the U.S. Department of State in Pretoria, South Africa, catalyzed the practical application of my academic studies. As an intern at the American Embassy I witnessed firsthand the difficulties of international cooperation and negotiation on science issues. Temporarily replacing and later assisting the Economic Section's science and technology officer, I conducted fieldwork to assess the status of biotechnology in the country, interviewing a range of actors from academia, industry, and nongovernmental organizations and from various departments within the South African government. Given my academic background in molecular biology and genomics, I was able to gauge the technological capacity of the nation's internal policy apparatus for differentiating genetically modified (GM) versus non-GM agricultural products. Furthermore, my studies in the social sciences provided the backdrop for these technological assessments, and my report was attuned to the indigenous intellectual-property norms and other cultural notions which would affect potential U.S.–South African science and technology agreements. It was this potential for collaboration and trade which was of greatest concern in Washington. South Africa, a country which uniquely straddles the boundary between the developed and developing worlds, continues to be considered the "foothold" for African development. Since returning to the States to complete my undergraduate degree, I am even more convinced that a positive biosciences evolution in South Africa has the potential to set a precedent for the continent and provide a valuable model for the rest of the developing world. In

October, I submitted a proposal for a U.S. Fulbright grant to return to the country for a period of up to one year and assist in this process.

I am currently immersed in the senior honors thesis, which is providing another stimulating opportunity to synthesize my interdisciplinary academic work. The thesis will explore the responses of American courts of law to reproductive technologies as they continue to destabilize traditional kinship notions by exploding the number of actors and procedural steps involved in the previously holistic act of human procreation. Law lag, a theory widely accepted in the legal community, suggests that the appropriate process by which such technologies are normalized within the law is slow and ponderous. However, the thesis will suggest a more complex involvement of the law, which is itself a technology through which society defines and defends its common values, as it meets another technology which presents and makes possible competing, nonnormative definitions. In the case of reproductive technologies, this clash is seen when science makes possible kinship scenarios that run counter to traditional notions of family constellations accepted both by society and under law. When courts address such scenarios in the areas of law bound up with making and contesting families, they discursively reshape kinship notions. It is clear from these cases that the law is certainly not lagging, but rather is saying something very explicit about the meaning of kinship in a technologically enabled reproductive world. The thesis will consider the significance of what courts are saying against the backdrop of traditional kinship notions, identify what principles consistently inform kinship discussions within the law, and chart the flow of influence between technology, law, and society over the shifting landscape of human reproduction.

In conclusion, for continuing study past my undergraduate years, I seek a field through which both science and values may be mutually accommodated. The law, and the institutions of courts, juries, and judges through which it is handed down, is viewed by most societies as the highest arbiter of cultural values and norms and is therefore the appropriate arena in which to grapple with the difficult, complex questions posed by new biotechnologies. I'd like to train in this field because I anticipate that the dilemmas posed by genetics will see resolution only in the law—perhaps the only space in which the equally important, but often divergent value systems of science and society can be mutually accommodated. I'd like to aid in bringing the immense possibilities of genetics into alignment with our affirmed democratic principles and with the liberty of every individual in mind.

Review by Sam Teller

This is an excellent essay. The writer has a clear and compelling thesis that she skillfully and succinctly weaves throughout her essay. While the historical introduction is longer than ideal, the payoff is worth it, as the writer explains the root of her intellectual passions. She discusses her interdisciplinary work at length. While some paragraphs are dangerously close to résumé summary, the writer effectively demonstrates why a law school should want her: she is intelligent, passionate, and skilled. Her clear writing allows her personal strengths to shine. After reading this essay, the reader can easily set the writer apart from the thousands of other essays out there. The writer is interested in two fields joined by law, the writer has experience to prove her acumen in these fields, the writer is engaged in serious independent academic studies of law, the writer has goals, the writer can write—in other words, the writer has demonstrated in exceptional fashion how she satisfies nearly every criteria a law school demands of its applicants.

GREG SCALLY

"Past things unforgotten help to shape the future." So read the giant white Chinese characters carved out of a volcanic black wall in

Nanjing. Skulls, shattered bones, and other distressing evidence of the Rape of Nanjing in the winter of 1937–38 lay nearby. I recall standing in a bleak rain, being saddened by the suffering, yet uplifted by the resolve, of the victims there.

I was in the midst of a journey rooted in a high-school assignment of Homer's epic *The Odyssey*. The choices Odysseus makes, such as deliberately eluding the pleasures of the starry-eyed lotus-eaters, seemed to suggest something about what humans are and how they ought to live. The adventurous Greek hero inspired me to search out who I was and how I ought to live. Through his story and other reading, I came to believe that trying to understand humankind, the "world out there," and the relationship between the two was the most important task I could undertake.

So I majored in philosophy. From Plato to Heidegger, I learned theories describing humankind, how we make sense of the world, and therefore what kind of people we ought to be and how we ought to be governed. From this experience I developed an interest in examining which sides of political issues seem to accord better with what I believe about humankind and what our moral goals ought to be. While eventually inducing that I wouldn't find conclusive answers to any of my philosophical questions, the illumination of the broader situation of humankind continues to inform my general sense of virtue, politics, and decision making.

After college graduation, I set out to teach English in China, and history and English in Guatemala, for several reasons. First, my growing interest in politics led to a desire to experience different political, legal, and social systems and to understand how behavior and attitudes are constrained in each. Second, I wanted to gain real fluency in both Mandarin Chinese and Spanish. Third, I wasn't convinced that the world needed another philosopher and thought that by living abroad I might be able to determine what the world needs that I can offer.

My time in China and Guatemala fulfilled all of my expectations. In both places, the education I received far outweighed the education

I provided. I read local, native-language newspapers alongside U.S. newspapers, noting their contrasting interpretations of events. I found the dissonance even deeper upon reading history texts in the native languages alongside those published in the United States. Mutual fear and misunderstanding seemed to pervade the relations between nations, and I found myself caught in the middle, trying to understand the cultural, historical, and political assumptions of both sides. In April 2001, when a U.S. spy plane landed on Hainan Island in China, I had a unique vantage point from which to view this bilateral distrust and suspicion between nations. Berated on the street by local Chinese on the one hand and encouraged by acquaintances back home to give the Chinese government a piece of "our" mind on the other, I began to wonder about and research what role international law plays in such situations. The legal confusions and problems raised by such confrontations seemed far-reaching and enthralling.

A trip to the Nanjing memorial of the Japanese military's atrocities in World War II strengthened my conviction that international law and relations between nations affect people's lives profoundly. There lay the gruesome results of shared cultural misunderstanding and fear. China closed itself off from the rest of the world for twenty-seven years shortly thereafter, but its recent entry into the WTO confirms its renewed embrace of global trade and broad diplomatic relations. Similarly, Guatemala's recent CAFTA negotiations with the United States highlight its belief that participation in the international community benefits its people.

Whatever the merits and shortcomings of globalization, these developments raise complicated and intricate legal issues in both the public and private sectors. From development lawyers who draft laws governing public fund allocation in Guatemala to corporate lawyers who consider local, regional, and treaty law in consulting on infrastructure-finance deals in developing countries, international lawyers possess unique skills that enable them to influence the way business and government operate. From State Department legal attachés who advise corporations expanding abroad, to human rights lawyers who attempt to ensure compliance with peace accords, international lawyers require a skill set I possess: language fluency, cultural understanding, analytical ability, and a sense of both progress and justice. I have concluded that what the world needs that I can provide is, in fact, the skilled efforts of one more attorney.

My odyssey has brought me through Aristotle and Nietzsche, Shanghai and Guatemala City. However, as with Odysseus, so with me: the "Great Wanderings" must come to an end at a meaningful destination. The Greek warrior sailed home to massacre 107 men and reclaim his wife. My ship, much less dramatically, is docking at law school, and with a keen eye on things past, I look forward to studying law to help shape the future.

Review by Nicholas K. Tabor

This author explores how he developed his interest in the law; it is a classic "why I want to be a lawyer" piece. Though it seems to merely show his professional motivations, Scally's essay demonstrates many important aspects of his personality in the process: his long-standing interest in questions of morality, his enduring intellectualism, his international flavor and willingness to dive headlong into issues that engage his passion, and his desire to work in a noble profession. Scally also briefly discusses international affairs through the Hainan Island and Nanjing stories; though he wisely keeps these discussions within the framework of why he wants to be a lawyer, they further show his interest in politics and his ability to analyze them in a more philosophical way.

However, mentioning particular political incidents is not always a wise choice. International espionage and incidents of genocide are complex geopolitical issues, and there isn't space to probe them fully in a personal statement. The result of trying to do so can come across as unreasoned and conceited; it may suggest that the applicant is not mature enough to recognize the intricacy of the questions at hand. Likely, this is the reason Scally inserts the phrase "whatever the merits and shortcomings of globalization" at the start of the seventh paragraph; he's telling the admissions officer that he doesn't intend to focus on the issues outside of his own narrative, but it's a bit of a wishy-washy tactic. Scally's language is also a tad melodramatic, such as his repeated use of the word "so" to begin sentences. He's writing a personal statement, not a Homeric epic, and he'd do well to use the appropriate tone for such an essay.

David Sclar

I believe that the nexus of health care and the law will be the backdrop for some of the most important decisions this and other nations will face during my professional career. In the decades ahead, health care systems will incorporate new technologies, scientific discoveries, public policy, and structural reforms. Lawyers will play a critical role in shaping the evolving health-policy context. With a sense of both excitement and responsibility, I anticipate that professional training in the law will provide me with the tools to make my greatest impact on health care issues.

For as long as I can remember, I have been fascinated by the capabilities of medicine and personally committed to the challenge of improving people's health. Upon entering my sophomore year at Harvard, I realized that my skills and interests were best suited to studying and eventually working in health policy as opposed to medicine. In the years since, I have engaged myself in a variety of academic disciplines, extracurricular activities, and employment where I have endeavored to influence health policy. I have found a passion for

An Intellectual Desire

health policy that has motivated my undergraduate and graduate studies and will continue to guide my pursuits in my legal career.

My experiences in my academic studies and employment have convinced me that legal training will allow me to have the greatest impact on health care. As a student of health policy, legal issues have threaded their way through my research: a paper for Professor John Akula on the role of the law in regulating the privacy of electronic medical records, an article I published in the *Harvard Health Policy Review* examining options for reforming the malpractice system, and my graduate thesis comparing policies to address medical errors in the United States and the United Kingdom. In my work experiences, I have witnessed the value of legal training in my mentors' successful health-care careers. I have readily identified with their intellectual energy, and I have seen how their background in the law enables them to address complex health-care issues.

I believe that I have similar professional and personal strengths that will make me a strong law student and lawyer. My intellectual interests motivate me to study legal theory and its practical application in society. My skills as a writer, a researcher, and an editor will allow me to write and think critically in law school and in my professional career. I am personally committed to valuing objectivity and fairness, promoting respect for others, and benefiting society in my work; these characteristics will ensure that I take pride in serving as an honest and respectable lawyer.

As I prepare for a career in law, my interests are both broad and directed. I am enthusiastic about the many directions my legal career may take me. At the same time, I know that I will remain dedicated to working in the health care field. A legal education will prepare me for a wide range of careers: as a practicing attorney, as well as in industry, academic research, and policy making. More importantly, a legal education will provide me with the professional skills to make my greatest impact on the issues that I know best and care most about.

Review by Shifra Mincer

David's essay succeeds in giving a clear and direct explanation of why he wants to attend law school. His interest in the nexus of health care and law is a theme that permeates the entire essay, and by the end his interests have expanded to include other possible applications of the law. This makes him a more attractive candidate because, while he has strong interest in one particular area, he is open to exploring others as well. Structurally, the essay is sound because it stays on topic, and has an argument that progresses smoothly from one paragraph to the next.

David's personal statement is a bit impersonal, and there are few personal anecdotes or images. This is usually unavoidable in essays that examine a particular legal issue, but in an essay that examines a personal interest in a field, you should look to include more anecdotes and images. David, for example, makes broad generalizations about people he has admired, but does not give any specifics about them. This lack of detail prevents the admissions officer from getting a real sense of the applicant from the essay.

David does a good job of emphasizing his strengths, explaining not only why he wants a law degree, but also why he would make a good lawyer. But he does not illustrate those strengths through anecdotes of how he has used them in the past. He says he is committed to objectivity and fairness, but never explains why or gives sufficient proof of this claim.

MOLLY SILFEN

My brow furrows as I shuffle tiles around, sticking the Z between the A and the E, and then pushing the D to the back of the line. With a sweeping gesture, I place FAZED where the F joins the word EN on a triple-letter score, and the *D* lands on a double-word score. "Sixty-six points," I declare triumphantly. "And I didn't even use all of my letters."

I have been playing Scrabble since I was eleven. When I was young, I watched my dad win game after game and finally convinced him to play me. At first he beat me soundly every time, but I could not get enough of the game. Week after week, I lost but continued to absorb strategies to make the most out of seven tiles. Four months after we began playing together, I eked out my first win, 313 to 294. My dad and I still play Scrabble together, diligently recording each of our scores and their sum to assess the overall quality of the game. These days I beat him just over half of the time.

I have always loved solving problems, and games have the kind of focused creativity that I enjoy most. A precise set of rules forces me to choose the best path within the game's structure. I can utilize my creativity and problem-solving skills in the quest for the honor of a hard-won victory.

In college, my love of problem solving led me to mechanical engineering. I soaked up the theories behind the problems and applied them to new situations. Like a player in a game, I followed given parameters and tried to design the best possible machine to fit a specified problem. For my senior project, for instance, I had to design a machine that tested the flexibility of a spine but fit within a foot of the wall, cost less than a thousand dollars, and applied no extraneous forces on the spine segment. After many wrong turns, I designed and built the working machine. Not only did I enjoy the process, but in the end my problem solving also improved the whole lab's ability to carry out its research. I was proud to have used my creativity in a meaningful way.

Engineering has a lot of the elements of games I have always loved, such as creativity within a framework and the need to strategize, but one key element is missing. When playing a game, the opponent is not static; it is a live person who can make mistakes and who also can amaze me with his or her ingenious plays. In an engineering problem, the human element is removed, and the face-off is often the engineer versus the laws of physics. Even though an engineering problem ultimately benefits an end user, as an engineer I rarely get to see my own impact on others.

Since working in a patent-law firm, I have realized that patent law can combine my problem-solving creativity with my engineering background and my preference for human interaction. I can use my engineering skills to understand the designs set before me. Law inherently involves working with others because it is constructed by society for the benefit of society. As an engineer, I revere the process of invention, and I am excited to help the world to place a greater value on its inventors and creators by protecting the intellectual property of others.

I have continued to play Scrabble for so many years because it is both dynamic and interesting—it requires that I constantly adjust my strategy to new situations. The law presents a similar challenge that I am eager to face—a series of problems that I hope and intend to solve. With the law serving as the rules of the game, I can use my creativity and problem-solving skills to make the most out of every set of tiles.

Review by Shifra Mincer

This is an extremely well structured and gripping essay that succeeds in convincing the reader that the candidate is passionate about law school and is qualified to study for the degree.

Silfen's introduction consists of an anecdote that is interesting and pulls the reader into her essay. The emphasis on her Scrabble skills allows her to highlight her strengths without simply stating them. Her detailed accounts of matches with her father keep the essay engaging and help to give the admissions officer a better sense of her character.

In the body of her essay, the candidate shows how she uses

her love for problem solving in other fields. Again, she uses specific examples of engineering problems she encountered in order to illustrate her points and keep her essay taut. She successfully explains why engineering is no longer her primary interest and why she turned to law instead. Although she risks exhausting certain cliches, such as the "helping the world" line in the second-to-last paragraph, Silfen does tie together her essay very well by the conclusion. She gives a concrete example of a possible career path in the law, explaining why she would enjoy it and why she would excel in it. By bringing back the images of playing Scrabble from the introduction, she ties the essay together neatly and succinctly.

The candidate is careful to use correct grammar, punctuation, and spelling, and her sentences read very easily and clearly. It is also very good that she completely avoided restating her résumé. She is an excellent Scrabble player, but this is not something that is written on her résumé. She is using the personal statement to highlight an accomplishment that would not otherwise be known to admission officers.

Lucy Stark

During the course of my chemistry doctoral research I have acquired an adeptness at analyzing chemical reactions, a keen eye for elegant molecular transformations, and a sharp ear for imminent explosions. What I regard as one of the most important developments of my Ph.D. studies, beyond my technical expertise and scientific accomplishments, is my passion for advocacy, as I strive to make a positive change in my own environment as well as for others in my community.

Upon entering the chemistry Ph.D. program at the Scripps Research Institute, I found myself in a department with only a handful of female students and no women faculty members. Since Scripps did not have an organization for women in science, I took the initiative to establish one myself, and thus the Network for Women in Science (NWIS) was born. I wrote letters to students and faculty to gauge and garner interest, met with professors to recruit their involvement, and solicited funding from the dean of the graduate school. By the time I stood at the front of a full auditorium and welcomed an audience of nearly one hundred people to our inaugural event, I had succeeded in bringing together a core group of students and faculty advisers whose enthusiasm was central to the sustained viability of the nascent association. Our first event consisted of a panel of four professors and a scientist from a local biotechnology company tasked with discussing issues that affect scientific career development. The panel turned out to be an enormously successful forum for airing issues especially pertinent to women in science and for building momentum for our future endeavors. I have since overseen the growth of NWIS into a full-fledged organization replete with bylaws, elected officers, a website, and financial backing from the graduate program.

My interest in activism has been influenced by my studies in both science and philosophy. As a college freshman I enrolled in a yearlong core philosophy class and was immediately captivated by the subject. My propensity for critically examining ideas often taken for granted was welcomed by my instructors, and I thrived on the heavy writing requirement inherent to philosophy curricula. As my studies progressed, I became increasingly fascinated with the interplay between philosophy and my burgeoning interest in chemistry. Through my classes in thermodynamics and quantum mechanics I quickly enmeshed myself in philosophical discussions with instructors and fellow students in the chemistry and philosophy departments alike. I read and reread physicist-philosopher Thomas Kuhn's seminal book *The Structure of Scientific Revolutions*, which so successfully bridged the subjects of philosophy and science that it became a source of inspiration and influenced my thinking across disciplines. In addition, my own independent research in the chemistry department fostered an insight into the daily details of scientific endeavors that informed my philosophical writings.

An Intellectual Desire

My philosophy training in turn nurtured an acute awareness of some of the assumptions surrounding the practice of science, such as the notion that observational data about the physical world are unassailably objective and thus impervious to subjectivity. Such a conviction tends to obscure the influence, however subtle, of the scientific practitioner's prior experiences or biases on the selection of research projects and methodologies.

These observations about subjective influences were pivotal in shaping my appreciation for how demographic distributions within the scientific community, in particular the underrepresentation of women, impact scientific practices and institutional dynamics. My desire to actively address the underrepresentation of women in science dates back to college and was precipitated by my experience as one of very few women chemistry majors. I joined the advisory committee of the Stanford Women's Science and Engineering Network (WSEN) and assisted in planning panels, receptions, and lectures by prominent women scientists. Upon assuming the leadership of the association, I initiated a mentorship program aimed at pairing up women undergraduates majoring in scientific disciplines with faculty members in similar fields. As a proponent of mentoring on a multitude of educational levels I also volunteered as a mentor and science tutor for Upward Bound, an organization serving high-school students who are the first in their family to go to college.

My involvement with WSEN and Upward Bound at Stanford and, more recently, with NWIS at Scripps has served to underscore my passion for advocacy and the importance of taking initiative and interacting with different people in order to translate theoretical musings into action. This, I have found, requires the ability to communicate effectively, as well as a bit of idealism, a whole lot of tenacity, and, to paraphrase philosopher John Rawls, a commitment to regarding others not as means only but as ends in themselves.

These experiences have contributed to my desire to concentrate on a career centered around advocacy and to take an active role in shaping the legal and policy decisions that affect society. I have had a fruitful experience as a scientist, yet I have also become cognizant of the multitude of aspects surrounding our daily lives that are influenced by regulations and policies that hinge upon an understanding of science, from laws regulating the purity of our drinking water to stem cell research. I am excited about pursuing a rigorous legal education and applying my multidisciplinary background to legal perspectives and objectives.

Review by Katherine M. Gray

Lucy explains how her passions for philosophy and chemistry collide with advocacy, which relates to her interest in law school. The essay serves as both a description of her many accomplishments as well as a demonstration of her ability to think and write about complex ideas.

Lucy could improve the essay by providing a concrete example of how she would bridge science and law. Also, some colorful anecdotes or details would showcase her personality; the essay now reads very academically.

Advocacy is a part of law, but not all of it. Lucy should describe how learning the legal code would benefit her in promoting issues that she cares about; specifically, the cause of women in science. She needs to show why she wants to be more than just a scientist with persuasive ability—why she wants a law degree in particular.

Lucy describes getting in front of a hundred people at her organization's inaugural event, but she doesn't describe feelings of anxiety or excitement she may have felt at that moment. She could also describe in telling detail how she "read and reread" Kuhn's book and how it inspired her. Getting across more of her human side in the essay would make it even stronger than it already is.

An Intellectual Desire

SANDRA PULLMAN

It had been during the Vietnam War, and the man had stared,
meanly and righteously. "The United States—how can you live in
that country?"
    Agnes had shrugged. "A lot of my stuff is there."
                           —Lorrie Moore, Birds of America

Living in Chile during the conflict in Iraq, another American war drawing heated international response, I've confronted the same scrutiny as Agnes. Even in the American-style high school at which I teach, the students and teachers from around the world are highly critical of the United States. One of my students in Journalism eyed me warily, as if I represented a global empire, when he handed in an article condemning the battle on Iraqi soil.

But the first assignment for my class, before attempting political commentary, was a simple interview. And their subject was the new teacher—me. I answered the typical questions about Harvard, about my travels around the world, and about my work in journalism, publishing, and creative writing. The students proceeded to nod agreeably and take notes—until they asked about my future plans. I saw the entire class bristle when I answered plainly: law school in the United States.

They really couldn't understand why, at first. Why, as a writer and a traveler, would I want to spend the next three years cloistered in a law library? Why would I return to my roots when my homeland was the source of ambiguous moral debate? I could tell they saw my destination as a fallback and my career choice as a cop-out.

But words are not merely decorative art, I tried to explain, nor is writing a craft that exists for its own sake. So rather than a consolation prize for failed novelists, law is in fact the most immediate application of a desire to write the texts that shape our lives. As for traveling, this hardly creates emotional distance from my origins, I insisted; ultimately, a traveler is always seeking out the qualities abroad that truly hit home.

On one assignment for the Women's Heritage Project, I recalled, I interviewed a woman who had documented the personal tragedies of the grandmothers of the Plaza de Mayo. I told her story and that of these women who had lost descendants in the Argentinean Dirty War as a testimony to human rights atrocities, even as our government and theirs were attempting to smooth over former involvement. Later on, when I traveled to Buenos Aires, I was amazed to discover the lasting scars of past policy as I watched these women and their daughters [in a] continuing weekly vigil in the city center.

I moved to London to study Shakespeare and European law, I told the class, both of which ultimately spoke to me as a New Yorker. I wrote a review of the female immigrant experience portrayed in *A Yiddish Queen Lear* for my Text and Theater course, and I compared the NYPD to the Elizabethan concept of justice in *Measure for Measure*. After interviewing a representative from the Collection of British Prostitutes for Criminology, I wrote a travelogue through Amsterdam about the red-light district's blurring of the boundary between sexual mores and personal freedom. I reflected not only on the Forty-second Street of my youth, but [also on] the models in Fifth Avenue windows today.

Even at work as an English teacher in Santiago, I've learned, words can carry the weight of social justice. Neither the anniversary of the Twin Towers attack nor the Pinochet coup was acknowledged at my school this September 11, as both issues involved not only victims of officially sanctioned "evil," but [also] political controversy on both sides. Despite the school's silent neutrality, however, I gave my own class a chance to discuss their emotional reactions to the events. And while I was many miles from Manhattan, I attended a tribute to Chile's mourning that week, listening to testimonies, songs, and poems in the same national stadium that had functioned as a torture chamber thirty years ago.

An Intellectual Desire

Writing is about addressing the human condition and giving form to collective values, I entreated my class. Meanwhile, travel stems from a desire to better understand these qualities, starting from the place one has left behind. And just as writing and traveling have taken me to distant lands, I reflected, both are now calling me home. My stuff is there, I told the skeptical sixteen-year-olds—and this had nothing to do with CDs or shoes or clothes in my closet, but rather with the fabric of my life. For despite all the moral ambiguities of the United States, I find that all my ideals and principles, my loved ones and formative institutions, are located in the details of American life—either as it exists today, or [as] I hope to shape it with my own words.

Review by Daniel J. T. Schuker

This essay succeeds largely because the author makes a compelling case that pursuing a legal career is consonant with her personal values and her identity. Although the logic of her choice is not immediately apparent to others, she is able to demonstrate the link between her past experience and her present choice. The introductory paragraph makes no references at all to the legal profession. And her first reference to law school prompts deep skepticism from her students. The author feels bound to justify why, "as a writer and a traveler," she would "want to spend the next three years cloistered in a law library." Her answer to her students is also her answer to the admission committee's question.

The thrust of the essay is to draw connections between the author's life experiences and her aspiration to attend law school. She does not claim that she has always wanted to be a lawyer, but rather that a career in law suits the interests that she has developed over time. As a writer and a teacher, she explains, she has come to understand that "words can carry the weight of social justice." As a traveler, she has become well attuned to the "moral ambiguities of the United States," yet she has also continually sought out "the qualities abroad that truly hit home." To make the connection concrete, she incorporates examples from her résumé, but not to the point of repeating it. The author weaves her identity as a writer and traveler into a coherent narrative in which, she argues, law school is the next logical step.

As a writer, she brings a special outlook on the law—her faith in "the texts that shape our lives." And as a traveler, she possesses a distinctive perspective on the nation in which she intends to practice law. She stands out from the crowd of Harvard Law applicants, she contends, because she will contribute to the school a unique understanding of the United States and the principles that underlie its laws.

DAVID PEARL

"David, when you are in Boston, you can have Thanksgiving with Grandma," my mother casually suggested, apparently failing to notice my eyes bulging in response. I had an idea about what she was insinuating but remained unsure until later that week, when my father made clear my parents' thoughts, prefacing a sentence with, "When you are at Harvard . . ." To give some background, both my father and brother attended Harvard Law School, my mom worked as my dad's legal secretary, and I had recently told them all that I had decided to go to law school. My parents had never pressured me to go to law school or to go to Harvard before, so, instead of feeling pressure from their comments, I felt somewhat amused at their haste and quite enjoyed lecturing both of them on "not counting one's chickens." The entire situation smacked of the absurd because I never thought I would ever want to go to law school, let alone apply to Harvard.

For as long as I can remember, an intense desire to be different has dominated my personality, and thus the thought of doing the same thing as everyone else in my family did little to excite me. This is why I had never entertained the idea of becoming a lawyer and why I abandoned my high school successes in the humanities to become a psychobiology major at UCLA, with the idea of going to medical school. I grappled with chemistry, biology, physics, and calculus for nearly two years before I had to face certain realities: I had had some success in science, especially biology and physics, but felt as if I had lost my way and decided to scale back and reassess what I wanted in life.

Midway through my sophomore year, I enrolled in my first college English class and bathed in the familiar glow of reading, writing, and research. My manic glee at taking a non-science class led me to believe I should quash the idea of medical school. Taking more English while continuing my science classes, I now toyed with the idea of pursuing a Ph.D. in either Biobehavioral Sciences or English. None of these ideas ever felt entirely right to me, largely because they failed to satisfy my desire to be different.

Choosing a humanities-based path or a science-based path made me uncomfortable because my straddling the chasm between the sciences and the humanities, enjoying different parts of each, and using them to complement one another largely satisfied my desire to be different. I felt this gave me a unique point of view, and did not want to give it up. Yet I had trouble finding a career in which I would not be forced to [do so].

Luckily, my brother came to the rescue, mentioning discussions he had been having with colleagues who repeatedly mentioned the importance of having lawyers with a science background in the future, given the increasing relevance of molecular biology and other sciences to the law. This did not mean much to me until I investigated the law and realized that much of what lawyers do revolves around reading, writing, and research. Finally, I had found a career path that would allow me to use the techniques of the humanities without having to abandon science. To my surprise, the law, which I had associated with sameness, turned out to be the vehicle by which I will be able to satisfy my own desire to be different and through which I might make a difference as well.

Being different, though extremely important to me, has always had to vie with another force: an urge to be the best I can possibly be. This urge led me to search for a law school with a stellar reputation for producing the best lawyers. It did not come as much of a surprise that Harvard fits those criteria, and, in one of the more surreal twists in my life, I now find myself eagerly applying to Harvard Law School. I guess my parents are just a few steps ahead of me. Well, more than a few, considering that lately they have started asking me what color I plan on painting the Oval Office.

Review by Andrew C. Esensten

In this essay the author attempts to explain why, despite his "intense desire to be different," he has decided to apply to his father's and brother's alma mater. The premise of the essay is good. However, Pearl takes the reader on a confusing tour of his academic career, pointing out landmarks without giving much background information. For example, he writes about how he reconsidered his plan to attend medical school after taking a college English class. What was the class about and why did he enjoy it so much? These are details that can make an essay really come alive.

The best personal statements are the ones in which applicants engage in self-reflection without drawing attention to the situation that prompted such reflection. In other words, the most memorable essays are the ones that have an organic quality, that don't sound manufactured for an application (even though they are).

To his credit, Pearl spices the essay up a bit with punchy prose such as "manic glee" and "surreal twists." Unfortunately, the essay clunks in a number of spots, including here: "Being different, though extremely important to me, has always had to vie with another force: an urge to be the best I can possibly be." Confident applicants shouldn't have to say that they always strive to be the best they can be; the admissions officers should be able to see that in the essay and . . . elsewhere in the application.

REBECCA MANGOLD

"Erika" was only four when she was placed in the foster care system after her pregnant mother tested positive for PCP. Though Erika was smart and did well in school, she became sexually active at an early age as a result of sexual abuse she had experienced as a child. When foster parents began to reject her because of her sexual behavior, she turned to prostitution as a way of surviving on her own. By age fourteen she had dropped out of school, lived on the streets, and undergone multiple abortions.

Erika was one of the many children I worked with at the Juvenile Intake Office of the Washington, D.C., Superior Court. I met with children like her on a weekly basis to help them overcome their self-destructive behavior, and referred them to rehabilitative programs so that their cases would not be sent to court. For children charged with more serious crimes, I conducted extensive interviews to obtain a comprehensive picture of their backgrounds, and wrote memorandums detailing my recommendations for each child's placement. At times, I argued for these recommendations in court over the recommendations of opposing attorneys who were oftentimes not as familiar with the entire case. Although working at the Superior Court was my first hands-on experience with juvenile law, I had been interested in children's legal rights ever since a serious crime was committed against someone close to me.

After seeing the devastation caused by Hurricane Mitch, I volunteered with "Amigos de las Americas," a program that works to promote sustainable development in Latin American countries. I lived in a small community in Honduras where it was normal for a family of fourteen to live on less than fifty cents a day. While I spent every day working with nearly all of the town's two hundred children, I developed the closest relationship with my thirteen-year-old neighbor, "Maria." Toward the end of my stay, Maria was raped by a local man. Her mother went to the police, who arrested the man but released him the next day because the family was unable to afford a lawyer. Because Maria was so young, the rest of the town dismissed her story, claiming that she was either lying or had brought it upon herself.

I remember seeing her mother collapsed and sobbing on the dirt floor, and the knot I felt in my throat as I held Maria with shaking hands. After that night, I knew that working to defend children like her had to be a part of my life. This experience motivated me to join the Board of Directors of Amnesty International, UCLA. In an effort to inspire more students to be involved in the fight against child sex abuse, we put on events publicizing children's rights issues, such as the child sex trade. Although there are over two million children in sexual slavery today, few laws exist that allow for the prosecution of such crimes, creating little pressure for change. We organized a weeklong event that incorporated film screenings, speakers (including a former child-slave from Sudan), and an active fund-raising campaign for groups that helped victims of child sex slavery. Through our efforts, we doubled group membership and raised more money than ever before with one event.

I have now had the opportunity to work with child victims of sexual abuse in many different contexts, and want to continue working on these and similar issues, especially at the international level. Each of the projects I did was rewarding, but I felt limited in what I was able to accomplish. I believe that a legal education will provide me with the tools necessary to create more substantive change. My experience at the Superior Court taught me that the legal system has the power to improve a person's life. When I last talked to Erika, she was finally happy living at home and had stopped having promiscuous sex. She passed a difficult test to enroll in a G.E.D. program, and now has dreams of becoming a firefighter.

Review by Casey Bi

Rebecca tells a compelling story here, tracing her different experiences with the victims of child sex abuse and using them to convincingly explain her desire to pursue the law. Her relationships with Erika and Maria lend emotional weight to her decision and arouse the reader's sympathies.

What is most impressive about this essay is that Rebecca avoids mentioning her own qualifications for law school—all of which is spelled out in the rest of her application—leaving the reader to discern her character and other personal characteristics from the way she tells her story and how she reacts to events. Rebecca's prose style is simple and clear and, as a result, keeps the essay moving briskly without becoming maudlin. Beginning and ending the essay with Erika unifies it while leaving the reader on a hopeful note.